What I Wish I Knew Before My 20th Birthday

Pathway to a successful life

NANA BEDIAKO BSN, RN, CCM

WHAT I WISH I KNEW BEFORE MY 20TH BIRTHDAY
Pathway to a successful life

Publisher
Royale Worldwide Publishing
www.royaleworlwidecorporation.com

First Edition
ISBN-13: 978-1-7322957-0-4 - E-book
ISBN-13: 978-1-7322957-2-8 - Paperback
ISBN-13: 978-1-7322957-1-1 – E-book - Smashwords
Printed in the
United States of America

Publishing Consultants
Vike Springs Publishing Ltd.
www.vikesprings.com

For Bookings and Speaking Engagements, Contact Us:
Royale Worldwide Corporation
Tel# 307-429-0129
Email: royaleworldwidecorp@gmail.com

Nana's books are available at special discounts when purchased in bulk for promotions or as donations for educational, inspirational and training purposes.

Limit of Liability/Disclaimer of Warranty

Dedication

This book is dedicated to my lovely wife Linda,
My daughters Jada and Eliana,
All my friends and family,
And finally, you.

Acknowledgment

With deepest gratitude, I wish to thank every person that the Lord has brought into my life and inspired, touched, and illuminated me through their presence, love, guidance, and pristine advice.

My profound gratitude to Rev. Reindorf Mantey who saw this great potential in me, guided me, and pushed me beyond my limits to write my first book. Thank you, Apostle Alexander Gray; you told me years ago about this era of my life.

For generously contributing and sharing your wisdom, I appreciate you, Franklin Allakpo and Jeanette Kyei Mensah.

There is an African proverb that says: when you see a turtle on a fence, it certainly did not get there on its own. There are many people, whom I can't even list, that have made a tremendous impact in my life. They have given me encouragement, spiritual guidance, advice, love, and so much more.

To Apostle Oswald Boafo, thank you for your weekly advice; you saw great nuggets of spiritual gifts in me. I learned great leadership and relational skills from you. Rev. Agyemang Duah, I grew spiritually hanging out with you; you taught me the need to study the word and pray always. Rev. Assifuah and family, thanks for our unique history.

To Rev. Assuo Mensah, thank you for all the encouragement and mentorship you gave me throughout the years. Rev. Mark Asante Manu, you were always there throughout every milestone of mine, thank you. Thank you, Apostle Dr. Kwabina Akufo, for your love and support. Pastor George Aboagye, I am very grateful for you.

To the members and leadership of the Apostolic Church USA, Royal Assembly, the Men's Movement, Witness Movement, all the Apostles, Pastors, Elders, Deacons, and Deaconesses—thank you all.

To Lady Vivian Ofori and all my ministry friends and colleagues, you have shown great love and support. You've been there through thick and thin. Love you all.

Team Bediako, thank you for your patience and for sending Dad off to take care of Kingdom businesses.

Finally, my Heavenly Father, without You—I am nobody.

Foreword

Life is like a soccer match; it is played in ninety minutes but can also go into overtime when the game becomes critical.

There are times when you can go down in the first half but win the match at the end of the ninety minutes or during overtime. Life is also in stages and, at times, can be compared to the life of a butterfly: its first stage is an egg, then it becomes a larva, it moves on to become a pupa (caterpillar), and then, finally, a butterfly.

This book is loaded with powerful insights that will be of tremendous blessing to every reader who cares to make amends or begin again. Minister Nana Bediako is a real blessing to the kingdom, and I recommend this book for everyone.

Live long and prosper as you go through this wonderful package.

Forward by **Rev. Asuo Mensah**
Founder and Senior Pastor of Love Embassy Worldwide,
TV and Radio Host at Multimedia Group Ghana.

Contents

Chapter 4 - Entrepreneurship   85

Chapter 5 - Investments   103

Introduction

*You do not become good by trying to be good, but by finding
the goodness that is already within you.*

Eckhart Tolle

I used to doubt my capabilities. This book contains some of
the keys that helped me break off the chains of self-doubt,
and I think it will help you too.

I am very excited; I thank God for leading you to pick up
this book and read it. For years, the Lord had laid this noble
burden on my heart to share my testimony and experiences
with you. My inspiration for this book came from my two
beautiful daughters: Jada and Eliana. I have always enjoyed
inspiring, motivating, and cheering them on to work very hard
in achieving their goals.

Martin Luther King Jr. said it well: "I want my daughters to be judged not by the color of their skin, but by the content of their character."

I want to share the knowledge that I have acquired throughout the years and the mistakes that I have made—which I don't want them to repeat. Most of these experiences have changed my life, and I know it will change your life too. I want to train my girls not to be limited by gender, but to be equipped to know that they can achieve anything that they set their minds to—and that they can achieve more than their parents.

> *A good person leaves an inheritance for their children's*
> *children, but a sinner's wealth is stored up for the righteous.*
> Proverbs 13:22 (NIV)

One of the greatest inheritances I can leave my children is knowledge: the blueprints to a successful life and sharing my life experiences. The fundamental principle is raising them in the fear of the Lord.

> *But seek ye first the kingdom of God and his righteousness,*
> *and all these things shall be added unto you.*
> Matthew 6:33 (KJV)

This is the ultimate wish of God for His children: get saved, live right, support His kingdom, and get rich.

Beloved, I wish above all things that you may prosper and be in health, even as thy soul prospereth.

3 John 2 (KJV)

When my oldest daughter was three years old, whenever she found it difficult to deal with a task, be it a homework or a game, she would cry and scream, "I can't do it." I would always tell her, "in this house, we don't say I can't do it; we always try, and if we don't succeed, we try again." Years later, I heard her saying the same quote to my youngest daughter. That touched my heart so much to realize that she has kept those words for years and actually made it part of her life as she journeys to the land of success.

And here is the prime condition of success, the great secret, concentrate your energy, thoughts, and capital exclusively upon the business in which you are engaged. Having begun in one line, resolve to fight it out on that line, to lead in it, adopt every improvement, have the best machinery, and know the most about it.

Andrew Carnegie

If you could turn back time, what are some things you would like to have achieved by now? What would you have done differently? What goals would you have set?

As you read on, you will unveil the answers to all these questions. You will also learn about the power of a changed mind, dealing with the fear of failure, the beauty of wisdom, understanding your purpose and potential, seed, the power of idea and imagination, creating value, how to build relationships, entrepreneurship, investment, giving, dealing with procrastination, and choosing the right job for the future. May the Lord grant you divine revelation about yourself and your purpose as you read this book. May you never lack. Amen.

CHAPTER 1
DISCOVERING YOUR POTENTIAL

In life, whatever you want to change must first begin with your mind. It doesn't matter your location, the house you live in, or the clothes you put on. **If you don't change your mind, nothing will change. The quality of your life is reflective of the quality of your mindset.**

Let's talk about **change of mind** - the place where you create what you want to see manifested in your life.

> *From that time on Jesus began to preach, 'Repent, for the kingdom of heaven has come near.'*
> Matthew 4:17 (NIV)

The word repent means a radical change of mind that results in a change of direction. The kingdom is already within you, but to assess it, you have to change your mind—or simply renew your thinking.

THE POWER OF A MADE-UP MIND

Free yourself from any self-doubt or any negative thoughts that question your ability to live life to the max. We are fearfully and wonderfully made in the image and likeness of God. *Say to yourself: it's time for a change!*

What have you fed your mind with? ***You are what you feed your mind.*** Begin to delete all the errors, and start to enter all the good stuff - by meditating on the word of God that clearly states how wonderful and gifted you've been created by God. Before the law of attraction, there was this Bible verse: As a man thinketh in his heart, so is he. You attract what you think.

> *Finally, brothers and sisters, whatever is true, whatever is noble, whatever is right, whatever is pure, whatever is lovely, whatever is admirable—if anything is excellent or praiseworthy—think about such things.*
>
> Philippians 4:8 (NIV)

These are some of the things the Bible admonishes us to think about.

What do you see? Robert G. Allen said: **"The future you see is the future you get."** What images do you have in your mind every day? Free your hard drive and begin to download

God's divine purpose for creating you. Are you ready to change your mind?

This woman—who had been bleeding for twelve year - made up her mind to go out that day. She made a radical move: no matter her limitations. The throngs of people would scare just about anyone to give up and go home. Let alone the stress she had to endure to even get to her miracle. She began to confess the idea and desire in her mind. What she envisaged was a healed woman: "If I may but touch the hem of His garment, I will be made whole."

> *And, behold, a woman, which was diseased with an issue of blood twelve years, came behind him, and touched the hem of his garment:*
> *For she said within herself, If I may but touch his garment, I shall be whole.*
>
> Matthew 9: 20-21 (KJV)

This woman used the power of her tongue with her made-up mind. She was confessing her breakthrough and surely had it.

THE PARABLE OF THE LOST SON

> *[11]Jesus continued: "There was a man who had two sons.*
> *[12]The younger one said to his father, 'Father, give me my share of the estate.' So he divided his property between them.*
> *[13]Not long after that, the younger son got together all he had, set off for a distant country and there squandered his wealth in wild living.*

¹⁴After he had spent everything, there was a severe famine in that whole country, and he began to be in need.
¹⁵So he went and hired himself out to a citizen of that country, who sent him to his fields to feed pigs.
¹⁶He longed to fill his stomach with the pods that the pigs were eating, but no one gave him anything.
¹⁷When he came to his senses, he said, 'How many of my father's hired servants have food to spare, and here I am starving to death!
¹⁸I will set out and go back to my father and say to him: Father, I have sinned against heaven and against you.
¹⁹I am no longer worthy to be called your son; make me like one of your hired servants.'
²⁰So he got up and went to his father.
But while he was still a long way off, his father saw him and was filled with compassion for him; he ran to his son, threw his arms around him and kissed him.
²¹The son said to him, 'Father, I have sinned against heaven and against you. I am no longer worthy to be called your son'."

Luke 15:11-21 (NIV)

The prodigal son thought: I am in the pen with pigs now, but I am not made to be here. I might be in this mess right now, but I don't belong here. Your current situation is definitely not your final destination. He came to a realization: he could be better than his present state. He made up his mind to go back to his father. He was broke—he had lost everything, but the very moment he made up his mind to go back home, the change started. This can be applied to any weakness, addiction, or sin in our lives.

As a little boy growing up in Ghana, West Africa, I would look through magazines and would fantasize about all the beautiful pictures of the United States that I would see. I also watched the movie "Coming to America." I always told myself that one day I would be in the USA. I had no family in the USA and no pen pals - but I had the images engraved in my mind. I saw myself walking on the streets of NY when I didn't even have a passport. I believed God, but I did not know how He was going to do it. What I needed to do was to speak things that are not as if they were. I believed in the power of "building castles in the air"; for me, it's building your world with your imagination.

My journey to the States was not easy. There were many obstacles I faced: applying for a visa, buying plane tickets, and even trying to find a place to live for when I arrived. In my mind, I was not going to give up. There were times I felt like giving up on my dream of flying to the States, but I had a made-up mind—and quitting was not an option. The challenges I had to overcome in the United States were numerous, but I was determined to make it with God on my side. You can create an achiever's mindset. Set aside some time every day to work on your mind.

And be not conformed to this world: but be ye transformed by the renewing of your mind, that ye may prove what is that good, and acceptable, and perfect, will of God.
Romans 12:2 (KJV)

I told myself many times I could never sing, let alone write or compose songs. I always preferred drama or poem recitals over singing in our church youth group, but my Youth Pastor Harrison Acheampong always encouraged me and pushed me to join the choir.

The first time I stood in front of a congregation, it was a youth anniversary, and I had to preach. I shook like a leaf for about 20 minutes; thank God, I did not wet myself. To say the least, I wasn't impressed with my performance, but most people came over and told me how great I was. I then decided to do more and learn the techniques of public speaking. Today, I have stood in front of huge crowds to preach or sing with no problem. I simply had to change my mindset.

There was this uncommon desire to pursue my dreams, to achieve and build, and to be able to leave an inheritance for my children's children. I was hungry to work for myself and also be a risk taker because I realized quickly it is way riskier not to take risks. For me, risk-taking is faith *(substance of things hoped for, the evidence of things not seen)*. Risk is not being sure if it will work but being ready to take a leap of faith.

The fear of failure is—and has always been—in our mind. This largely outweighs our desire to succeed. To do something you've never done, you have to become someone you've never been. You have to take a chance and know that the failures or mistakes you make are a chance for you to find a way to make it better. Many inventions came out of the junkyard of failure or shameful mistakes.

In the journey called life, the one who started and failed

on the way is always better than the one who never tried. The first exams I ever failed really took a toll on me. I was very disappointed but quickly gathered myself together and reregistered for a second try. By the second trial, my confidence was stronger. I felt very comfortable because I was familiar with the exam room, set up, type of questions, and the timer. It took me way less time to complete, and I passed with a very high score.

An experiment was conducted with two rats (let's call them Rat A and Rat B). For a period of time, Rat A was placed in a container of water for a few seconds daily. The rat struggled each time it was placed in the water. After a week, both rats were placed in the container; Rat A survived while Rat B sunk. Water is not a natural habitat for rats, but after a while, Rat A had gained experience by honing and yanking on its survival instincts and tactics, which enabled it to stay in the water for a longer period of time than Rat B. "Experience is not what happens to an individual but rather what one does with what happens to them."

Fleming was researching for a "wonder drug" that could cure diseases. Ironically, it wasn't until Fleming threw away his experiments that he found what he was looking for.

Fleming was so eager to go on vacation, he left a pile of dirty petri dishes stacked up at his workstation before he left town. When he returned from his vacation on September 3, 1928, he began sorting through his pile of petri dishes to see if any could be salvaged. He discovered that most of them had been contaminated—as you might expect in a lab.

As has been well-documented in history books and on the Nobel Prize website, Fleming dumped most of the dishes in a vat of Lysol. But one of the dishes, containing staphylococcus, had something interesting in it.

The dish was covered in colonies of bacteria, except in one area where a blob of mold was growing. Around the mold was an area free of bacteria, as if the mold had blocked the bacteria from spreading. He realized it could be used to kill a wide range of bacteria—and penicillin was identified.

From that minor act of scientific sloppiness, we got one of the most widely used antibiotics today.

The **Wright Brothers Wilbur and Orville** were American inventors and pioneers of aviation. In 1903, the Wright brothers finally succeeded, after many failed attempts, in manufacturing the first powered, sustained, and controlled airplane; they built it on their own innovation. Two years later, they built and flew the first fully practical airplane. Through their failures, they were able to finally achieve their dream. The brothers started their careers as printers, started selling and later manufacturing bicycles, and then finally, started selling their aircrafts.

Thomas Edison famously quoted: "I have not failed; I've just found 10,000 ways that won't work." Failure does not mean the end; it should mean a lesson that will better prepare us for the next level. Edison tried the light bulb many times before he succeeded; he could have given up, but as he continued to fail, he was able to get rid of processes that did not work. Failure for God's children is not failure; rather, it's an opportunity to build faith in and with God.

That being said, the society in which we live does not honor failure. One of the best ways to foster innovation or learn is through mistakes. Failures are pivotal moments that urge us to take a different path to a better place.

But as it is written, Eye hath not seen, nor ear heard, neither have entered into the heart of man, the things which God hath prepared for them that love him.
1 Corinthians 2:9 (KJV)

There is greatness in you: jump and grow wings while you're falling down. Don't be afraid to jump out of the plane and open the parachute. If there's a defect, open the backup chute.

Be hungry to change your life: someone's opinion about you does not have to become your reality; it only becomes real if you accept it as truth.

Politician Robert G Allen said: "Don't let the opinions of the average man sway you. Dream, and he thinks you're crazy. Succeed, and he thinks you're lucky. Acquire wealth, and he thinks you're greedy. Pay no attention. He simply doesn't understand."

I remember an incident that happened about 25 years ago in Ghana. Students are required to take an entrance exam before going to high school, which they have to pass. Prior to the entrance exams, students are required to pick which high school they wish to attend. Students are expected to choose three schools. Every student meets with the headmaster or headmistress (principal) of their schools to fill out the forms for the schools which they have chosen. I picked three schools: my first choice was Mfanstsipim School, which is one of the elite schools in Ghana. Former General Secretary of the UN Kofi Annan attended this school. After I had finished filling out the forms, I left to go home. On my way home, I met a very close family friend who asked me where I was coming from. I told her about the activity at school, which included picking the schools we wanted to go to. She then went on to ask me what schools I chose. I listed all the choices, and she said, "Wow. All the schools you've picked are highly competitive schools. Do you think you can make the required grades to make it into those schools? You better go and change your selections." (Be careful who you share your dreams with. Some people are dream killers.)

I thought about it—and believed in the lies that she spoke to me. I turned back to meet with my headmistress to make changes to my selections. She was very upset but gave me White-Out to make the changes. I made the changes to a lower level set of schools. As I left her office on my way home, deep down in my heart, there was a sense of uneasiness. A few meters away from my house, I heard a voice behind me say… (Isaiah 30:21 - And thine ears shall hear a word behind thee, saying, this is the way, walk ye in it, when ye turn to the right hand, and when ye turn to the left or to the right.)

"Nana! Why have you made Me so small? Is there anything too hard for Me?" Suddenly, I started confessing: I can do all things through Christ who strengthens me (Philippians 4:13). I shall be the head and not the tail (Deuteronomy 28:13). I will bring to your remembrance all that you have learned (John 14:26). Call upon Me, and I will answer and show you the unsearchable things (Jeremiah 33:3).

I do not know how I ran all the way back to my school without talking to anyone on the way. That day was also the deadline to submit school choices or any other corrections. As soon as I entered my headmistress's office, I knelt down and begged her to please let me change my schools again. For those of you from Africa, you can imagine the fear. She was furious! I went and pleaded with another teacher—who is my godmother—to plead with my headmistress.

Finally, the headmistress decided to give me my forms to make the final corrections. My forms looked very ugly because there were multiple uses of White-Out and inks. After the correction, I went home without making any detours or stopovers. I did not mention the changes to anyone. However, some of my colleagues heard about the many changes I made on my forms from a student who was working in the office that day. Most of my classmates also told me I can never get into that school. Did I have doubts? Yes! I was not sure if I could make it into that school. I was beginning to believe in the opinion of this "evil" cloud of witnesses.

I had no idea that God was allowing all this negativity to prepare me for greatness. Most of my success had come from betrayals and people questioning my abilities and telling me I would never make it.

A week before our final exams week, I was infected with chicken pox. Oh God, why? I prayed. I could be kept out of the exams because it is very contagious. At the brink of starting the exams, I was not only totally healed, but I was determined to sit for my papers. I did not sleep well because of the infection, and l was staying up all night during the week of the exam. Most of my friends did not know what I was going through and might be reading this for the first time.

Because I was having sleepless nights, I was able to stay up for hours studying. I would go to the exam hall but would not feel any weakness: I was all set for my exams. God granted me favor, strength, a nimble mind, and a passion in my heart to drive me on.

> *For the vision is yet for an appointed time;*
> *But at the end it will speak, and it will not lie.*
> *Though it tarries, wait for it;*
> *Because it will surely come, It will not tarry.*
> Habakkuk 2:3 (NKJV)

A couple of months after the exams, the results were out. I came out with flying colors—the highest aggregate score ever in that school. Finally, I was able to make it into the best school in Ghana, which was my first choice.

All my friends came over to congratulate me. The news spread through the entire neighborhood; indeed, this church boy has proven that it's always good to serve God.

Trust me; there's nothing you cannot do. A positive mental disposition and a strong expectation of good things happening to you every day will make you nothing but a victor in life.

> **Believe in God, believe in yourself, and do not accept the opinion of others.**

Hard work will always pay off; all things will work together for our good. Always strive for the best because the best revenge is success. Work on what you feed your mind with. I pictured myself going to that school. My expectation was never cut off.

If you read biographies of most of the successful people in the world, you realize that the majority of their achievements came under very harsh conditions or experiences. Beethoven wrote and directed his most memorable symphony after he had gone completely deaf. Look at the beautiful songs written and sung by Stevie Wonder and Ray Charles. Indeed, no handicap is really an excuse for not achieving your dreams. Determination will bring us to the land of destiny.

Abraham Lincoln is the epiphany of the meaning of persistence. Many years after his death—and he is still mentioned as one of the best presidents to ever lead the

United States. I admire his tenacity to pursue his dreams and never give up. He was born into poverty. Throughout his life, he had to deal with defeat and huge obstacles. He lost many elections, failed in business twice, and was bedridden for months at a time, multiple times. He lost many loved ones, including his mother. He had little formal education but was involved in self-education. All indications proved that he would never be successful, but he was very determined and never gave up. Finally, he became the president of the greatest country in the world.

THE BEAUTY OF WISDOM

Wealth and success are in wisdom. We can't do without wisdom, knowledge, or understanding. I define wisdom as "the quality of having experience; being able to discern or judge what is true, right, or lasting and applying the information thereof to problem-solving." There are people who have great knowledge but are not wise. *Wisdom is the practical application of knowledge.*

Let's look at some scriptures:

> *[13]Blessed is the one who finds wisdom and the one who gets understanding, [14]for the gain from her is better than gain from silver and her profit better than gold. [15]She is more precious than jewels, and nothing you desire can compare with her. [16]Long life is in her right hand; in her left hand are riches and honor. [17]Her ways are ways of pleasantness, and all her paths*

are peace. ¹⁸She is a tree of life to those who lay hold of her;
those who hold her fast are called blessed.

Proverbs 3:13-18 (ESV)

According to this scripture, if you have wisdom, it will give you long life, riches, and honor. Someone with great wisdom will know market trends and how to invest. It's never a wonder King Solomon became the richest man in the world; his story is familiar to most people. In 1 Kings chapter 3, the passage talks about how King Solomon acquired his riches. Solomon asked for what was absolutely essential for him.

⁸And your servant is in the midst of your people whom you have chosen, a great people, too many to be numbered or counted for multitude. ⁹Give your servant, therefore, an understanding mind to govern your people, that I may discern between good and evil, for who is able to govern this your great people? ¹⁰It pleased the Lord that Solomon had asked this. ¹¹And God said to him, 'Because you have asked this, and have not asked for yourself long life or riches or the life of your enemies, but have asked for yourself understanding to discern what is right, ¹²behold, I now do according to your word. Behold, I give you a wise and discerning mind so that none like you has been before you and none like you shall arise after you. ¹³I give you also what you have not asked, both riches and honor so that no other king shall compare with you, all your days. ¹⁴And if you will walk in my ways, keeping my statutes and my commandments, as your father David walked, then I will lengthen your days.'

1 Kings 3:8-14 (ESV)

Solomon didn't care much for wealth but asked for wisdom. God added wealth, and his days were lengthened. Wisdom is really the key to wealth. Solomon's wealth and fame sprung from his desire to learn how the world works, which led to the smart choices he made in investments. You will be surprised to find out the number of people who have gone broke after they have won millions through the lottery. You can inherit or win a lot of money, but if you lack wisdom, you will end up broke.

> *By your wisdom and your understanding, you have made wealth for yourself, and have gathered gold and silver into your treasuries.*
>
> Ezekiel 28:4 (ESV)

Time and energy are wasted when a tree falls with a blunt ax. God expects us to work, but He wants us to work smarter and skillfully. Sharpen your life ax. This will make you use less effort and strength; it's, therefore, wise to get information in any venture you plan to go into.

A few areas that we all need to master are learning how to do some bookkeeping, how to invest or how investments work, the stock market, tax laws or tax benefits, and how to let your money work for you. We will touch on a bit more when we get to the investment chapter.

> *Poverty and disgrace come to him who ignores instruction, but whoever heeds reproof is honored.*
>
> Proverbs 13:18 (ESV)

Humility and readiness to learn is a prerequisite for increasing wisdom. Knowledge is power. Investing in books and information that are in line with your goals will prepare you and propel you faster to your destination.

In his book, "Becoming a Millionaire God's Ways," Dr. C. Thomas Anderson shared a story. The story is told of a man who, upon his retirement, was turning his business over to his son. He gave a few words of advice on his last day: "Son, what makes this business successful is reliability and wisdom. Wisdom understands the need of your customers. Great customer service skills and reliability are important. When you promise to deliver, be true to your word. These are great skills to have as a business owner or entrepreneur."

Now that we have touched a bit on renewing the mind, let's continue on **DISCOVERING YOUR POTENTIAL.**

VISION AND DREAMS

The greatest tragedy that can befall any man is not death, but a life without a purpose, vision, or dream—having eyes but not being able to see. Imagine how sad it would be to be alive and not know why.

Let's talk a little bit about vision. Malcolm Forbes said: "When you cease to dream, you cease to live." Joseph's voyage to greatness started with a dream from God about his future (purpose). For as a man thinks in his heart, so is he. As soon as Moses understood his vision, he began to realize his abilities.

Vision is seeing the end at the beginning. Every child has a vision. Kids speak very big. They come into this world with big dreams—until they share with their parents or a family member, and then, it gets killed.

Vision previews our purpose in life.

When I first came to the United States of America as a new and very young, undocumented immigrant, anytime I saw homeless people, some holding cards begging for money on the streets, others at the grocery store corners drunk, and those walking around aimlessly, I always would say to myself: I wish I had their social security number or citizenship—I would do a lot with it.

Why? I had lots of dreams coming to the States but did not have the proper legal documents that would underwrite my stay to enable me to pursue my dreams. Tuition fees were a difficult thing to raise. As a non-documented student, you do not qualify for any financial aid. I also did not have anyone to cosign for me to get any aid for school. It took me quite some years to get my residency and then be able to start school.

There are people with great opportunities at their disposal, but they lack purpose. When you die, you will be accountable for every minute you lived and everything you did with your life. By age 40, I had gained a lot of experience, clearly understood my purpose, and also realized that my greatest asset is my time. I wish I would have known these things when I was still in my young 20s. Now, in view of this new mindset, I live daily not wanting anyone to waste my time.

These are 3 essential keys that your dream will really need:

1. Write down your dream/vision, and make it easy to understand (Habakkuk 2:2).

2. Guard, read, and pray on your vision, and also, study or learn every day (John 10:10).

3. Maintain focus on your dream, always (Philippians 13:13).

Purpose is defined as the reason for which something is done or created or for which something exists. You and I are created for a purpose. The universe was created for a purpose, the garden of Eden was created for a purpose, Saul was met by Jesus for a purpose, and Jesus had a purpose for coming into this world ("For the Son of Man came to seek and to save the lost." Luke 19:10 NIV).

There were millions of sperm that were competing, but only one made it. Why did all of them die so only you would survive and be born? You are not here by mistake.

> **We are created to live life with a purpose—until the quest for our purpose is achieved, there will be no satisfaction.**

Myles Monroe said: "We are all created for a purpose, equipped with potential, and designed for destiny."

Any automobile manufacturer that has an intention to make a vehicle, of course, has a manual for the vehicle. To find our purpose, we have to go to the Creator.

What unique gift or talent do you have? What comes to you easily or naturally? What interests you so much that you can't seem to get your mind off of it? What makes you angry? These questions help identify your purpose. Mentorship is one of the things that make me happy. I love to teach, guide, and help people. If it took me years to get to a place in life, and I have the opportunity to guide someone to make it with a lesser number of years, then I should guide them. That is always great.

It's a pleasure seeing people succeed and being part of helping people climb the ladder of success. If I have had the spotlight in the past, I will not be selfish. I would love for someone with the same passion and potential to be there too. I feel that God will bless me so that I can be a blessing unto others. If I can do that with the small things that He's given me, then He will put me in charge of many. I do believe many people have died or die every day in most poor regions of the world due to the lack of simple CPR and First Aid.

Going out of your way to solve problems has a way of influencing your thinking and also helps birth your dream and vision.

> **Goliath was a big problem, but he became an opportunity for David's purpose.**

David was not important until he killed Goliath. Moses solved the problem of slavery. Businesses are also created by solving problems. You are one of a kind—wonderfully made by God with something unique. God does not create duplicates. That's why your DNA and fingerprint are unique just to you.

What qualities do you have that attract others, or what qualities do you have that people love? There are people who are able to make friends easily. That's a unique gift. Some people are naturally good in administration: putting things in great order, customer service, organizing excellent events, or managing things very well. How do you develop these skills that you have? I realized that I love public speaking; sometimes I'm the Master of Ceremony at events. People always told me that I am a great motivator and can capture the audience when I preach. I identified that gift and began to develop and work towards it.

You might love to cook or bake. You can prepare lots of different dishes at the same time with great joy and flair because you love it. That can be a purpose: a unique gift. You may have been told many times to start a business, but you're always procrastinating. You are sitting on a gold mine while praying for God to bless you financially. Invest in yourself.

You can even begin with a food truck; find out how to get the state license and the documents you need to file. You need to take the first step, and God will bring you divine helpers—just start. I know if you start, it will bring you great fulfillment.

Let's look at the life of Joseph in Genesis 39:3-5, 40:7-8, 41:15-16, and 41:39-41. He had only two unique gifts: managing the household and interpreting dreams. Same gift but different levels. The same gift made room for him and created success. He served his brothers, took food to them on the field, managed Potiphar's house, interpreted a prisoner's dream, the king's dream, and finally, his managerial gift led him to manage almost every resource in Egypt. Whatever you do or touch, ask God to make you fruitful.

As soon as you identify your purpose, you are able to discover your **POTENTIAL**. "The wealthiest place on the earth is not the huge diamond mines in South Africa or Rwanda; the rich gold mines in Obuasi, Ghana; the oil fields in Saudi; or the rubber plantations in Liberia, but it's the cemetery," said Dr. Myles Munroe. The graveyard is filled with ideas, visions, dreams, businesses, and inventions: all of these are called Potential.

POTENTIAL is defined as dormant ability, untapped power, hidden strength, reserved energy, capacity, or unleashed talents. There are massive abilities in us, which haven't been known or used yet. Once you've done something, it's no longer a potential.

Myles Monroe said: "The greatest enemy of your progress is your last success."

> **Don't settle for where you are now.**
> **God is waiting for more, and the world**
> **is counting on us to make an impact.**

We are not finished. We are just starting; potential is never finished, and we are bigger than what we are now. Before we even start the journey, God has already completed it. All things work together for our good. The fact that you lost your job was a set up to make you start your own business. There is a business potential in you that is yearning to manifest. Potential (ability to perform) is a product of purpose (why a thing is created).

God does not accept excuses because He sees the potential in you. Moses' excuses did not work because he was a deliverer by purpose and had the potential to lead. His leadership quality was nurtured when he lived with Jethro. Mary and Gideon's excuses did not work either because He created them and knew them even before they were born. Caleb saw his purpose and, therefore, was able to identify his potential. David was not among the chosen by his father, but God had a purpose for him. There was a potential to kill Goliath, but he had to develop his gift in the wilderness by protecting his sheep.

> **If God calls you, it means He has already deposited in you the unction to function.**

And the earth brought forth grass, and herb yielding seed after his kind, and the tree yielding fruit, whose seed was in itself, after his kind: and God saw that it was good.

Genesis 1:12 (KJV)

God placed the seed of everything He created within itself. Whatever God wanted the created item to be, He placed it in the item at the time it was created.

While the earth remains, seedtime and harvest, cold and heat, winter and summer, day and night, shall not cease.

Genesis 8:22 (ESV)

Adam was the first seed of the human race; through him, the earth was populated. God's intent is for us to be a blessing to others. Mandela's fight was not about him but to break his people free from the shackles of apartheid.

[8]Remember this and stand firm, recall it to mind, you transgressors, [9]remember the former things of old; for I am God, and there is no other; I am God, and there is none like me, [10]declaring the end from the beginning and from ancient

times things not yet done, saying, 'My counsel shall stand, and
I will accomplish all my purpose.'

Isaiah 46:8-10 (ESV)

God allows us to see the end from the beginning, which is called Vision. We are special in the sight of God. With His uniqueness, He places creative abilities in us, which push us to want to live a fulfilled life through understanding our assignment on earth.

The things that we see with our naked eyes are temporal; what you saw (vision/dream) is the purpose.

POWER OF AN IDEA

Now let's dive into the **Power of an Idea. An Idea is defined as** a thought or suggestion to a possible course of action, a concept or mental impression, the aim or purpose. An idea is very powerful; it produces everything around us, from creation to human inventions. The light bulb, ships, planes, buildings, weapons, computers, and the Internet all began with an idea.

Logos (Greek: "word," "reason," thought' or "plan").

In the beginning was the Word, and the Word was with God,
and the Word was God.

John 1:1 (KJV)

We can also say in the beginning was the thought, and the thought was with God, and the thought was God. In the beginning, God thought and spoke the thought into being and reality. As a man thinks in his heart, so is he. It's not about what people think about you but what you think about yourself. God will work on your thought and not what others think about you.

> **There is no limit to what God will do if your thoughts are right. If you can see the invisible, you will do the impossible.**

¹Blessed is the one
who does not walk in step with the wicked
or stand in the way that sinners take
or sit in the company of mockers,
²but whose delight is in the law of the Lord,
and who meditates on his law day and night.
³That person is like a tree planted by streams of water,
which yields its fruit in season
and whose leaf does not wither—
whatever they do prospers.

Psalm 1:1-3 (NIV)

This man thinks about God (divine ideas) every day. Therefore, his life is beautiful, and whatever he does, he prospers.

God had an idea to create the universe and man; for He said, let us make man in our own image and likeness. It was an idea. An idea cannot be destroyed; the person with the idea can die, but the idea will still leave on. People die and leave their ideology, which other people come to follow or enforce. Osama Bin Laden is dead, but his radical ideology still exists today, not saying it is good.

We are the thought of the Creator, created in His image; therefore, we have creative abilities in us to create things. God did not create furniture, but He created big trees, which furniture can be created from. Adam was placed in the garden to be creative. God instructed Noah to build an ark (big boat). He saw a boat in a big tree; he saw something different.

Create your own thought. God created us to be creators like Him. The planes, ships, cars, computers, houses, Facebook, Twitter, Amazon, etc., were not created by God, but He provided the raw materials for us to create those things. We are creators; you are the one who can create that medicine or that great technology which will save the world.

> **"Necessity is the mother of inventions." Most creations are born out of problems. Problems birth creativity.**

Prayer: God, please give me a thought, an idea, a plan and strategy to solve problems. A solution to the problem will birth a business, which can create wealth.

I love this interesting statement: "Take away everything I have but leave me with my mind. I will get it all back." One of the most expensive properties is our intellectual property because it can be used to create the kind of world we live in.

Philo Taylor Farnsworth was the official inventor of the first fully functional, all-electronic television. **Alexander Graham Bell** (1847-1922) was the Scottish-born American scientist best known as the inventor of the telephone. **Garrett A. Morgan** is an African American who invented traffic lights. All of these inventions started with an idea.

Dr. Wernher Von was one of the most important rocket developers and champions of space exploration in the 1930s. President J.F. Kennedy asked Dr. Von: "What will it take to build a rocket that will carry a man to the moon and safely bring him back to earth?" Dr. Wernher, in just five words, said: "The will to do it." They didn't know how to get it done, but they were very optimistic.

Andrew Carnegie said: "Any idea that is held in the mind, that is emphasized, that is either feared or revered, will begin at once to cloth itself in the most convenient and appropriate form available." Andrew Carnegie was a Scottish-American industrialist who led the American steel industry in the late 1800s. Rags to riches story, he sparked and stimulated philanthropy; his goal was to work very hard, make lots of money, and give it out. He donated about 350 million of his wealth. When God blesses you, don't forget to be a blessing.

One of the greatest and creative faculties that we possess is the power of our imagination.

> **Our imagination is bringing the future to the present and working on fulfilling it.**

Always picture yourself where you want to be.

William James said: "Act like the person you want to become by using your imagination." (I call this building castles in the air.) Every child has an imagination until they go to school and it is shut down. Parents, regardless of how stupid the idea might sound, let's support our children in the pursuit of their imagination (it can create wealth and fulfillment).

Naveen Jain is an entrepreneur, a billionaire who came from India to the United States with nothing and now has everything. This is what he said, and I love it: "When you share an idea with people, and they say you are crazy, that's too big for you, that's when you know you are doing something good and bigger." God wants variety and something new. God's vision for us is always bigger than us and causes us to solely rely on Him.

How do you want to live? Have that picture in your mind always. God asked Abraham to look up into the sky, to have a mental picture of what his descendants would look like. That mental picture guided his path to his destiny and fulfillment.

Exercise your imagination daily, build beautiful images in your mind (as a man thinks in his heart, so is he) about how you want your life to be and what you want to achieve. Wherever you want to go, begins with the first step. You don't need everything to start; you just have to start and then become the best with time.

Planning to get to the top? Then you have to let go of certain old bad habits. It's difficult to scale a high mountain with lots of baggage. To save energy, you have to take along the most valuable items, like water and some food. You don't want to carry pillows, jewelry, heavy books, or a computer that will weigh you down.

> [13]*Brothers and sisters, I do not consider myself yet to have taken hold of it. But one thing I do: Forgetting what is behind and straining toward what is ahead,* [14]*I press on toward the goal to win the prize for which God has called me heavenward in Christ Jesus.*
> Philippians 3:13-14 (NIV)

To win, you have to let go of any past events that will keep you from focusing on your goals. Always **feed your focus and starve your distractions.** That is the weapon the devil uses most of the time against God's children.

Find something that you are good at, and put all your focus on it. When I was a little boy, my friends and I would use a magnifying glass in the sun and focus it on a paper to light it. Focused attention is powerful. As you start focusing on your dream and goals, divine helpers will begin to come from places you had no idea.

> **That which we focus on, give attention and our energy to, will begin to multiply, expand, and shape us into bringing to pass our purpose.**

Put yourself in a position where you can't retreat: no retreat, no surrender; do or die. Put everything you've got into your goals and dreams. **You are the star of your own show—you're directing.**

Winston Churchill said: *"Courage is going from failure to failure without losing enthusiasm."*

> **Winners ignore their negative critics.**

See yourself every day as if you have very limited time on earth; what would you do if you only had a few months to live?

In the movie "Last Holiday," starring Queen Latifah and directed by Wayne Wang, Latifah plays a humble store assistant, Georgia, who is told that she has a rare brain condition and only a few weeks to live. She decides to spend her last funds on a luxury holiday in Europe before she dies. Free of inhibitions and determined to live life to the fullest, Georgia checks into the presidential suite, buys a designer wardrobe in expensive boutiques, makes extensive use of the hotel's spa facilities, attempts snowboarding, enjoys succulent meals prepared by world-renowned Chef Didier (Gérard Depardieu), and wins a small fortune playing roulette in the casino.

Finally, she realizes she was misdiagnosed due to X-rays generated by a broken, outdated CAT scanner. Queen Latifah did many things that she had dreamed about, which she would not have done if she hadn't received that deadly news. Learn how to block negative thoughts out, and write down your ideas every morning—which you can use to change your life. You will be surprised what will come out of that.

What can you do best? Develop your unique gift. The human spirit is very powerful; winners ignore their negative critics.

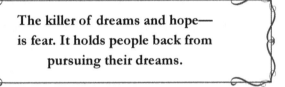

**The killer of dreams and hope—
is fear. It holds people back from
pursuing their dreams.**

Zig Ziggler said: "Fear is false evidence appearing real."

*And after you have suffered a little while, the God of all
grace, who has called you to his eternal glory in Christ, will
himself restore, confirm, strengthen, and establish you.*

1 Peter 5:10 (ESV)

Tough times never last but tough people do. Our deepest fear is not that we are inadequate; our deepest fear is that we are powerful beyond measure. The chapters in our life are still being written by the Author and Finisher of our faith, so don't give up; you are destined to win.

CHAPTER 2
CREATING VALUE

Value is simply what a thing can be traded for: the weight and importance placed on something. Most successful people, or those at the pinnacle of their field, all tend to have something in common. It will interest you to know that they invest most of their time adding value to other people's lives in some way, which inversely creates success for themselves.

> **One of the most powerful success strategies is creating greater value for others.**

By doing so, you increase your own value, or you become more valuable to them. Are there important people in your life? Are they directly or indirectly adding value to your life? Is your closeness to them making them contribute to your life? Emotionally, physically, spiritually, or financially? Are they building your self-esteem, celebrating, or cheering you on your success path? The value in a business relationship is mostly measured by your ability to do great business or the positive impact you have on your down line.

In the area of ministry, are you giving birth to your kind, that is, are you raising other leaders who will take over after you and not be intimidated?

> *Kind words can be short and easy to speak, but their echoes*
> *are truly endless.*
>
> Mother Teresa

There are billions of people on earth; among all those people, you are unique and wonderfully made by God. What makes you different and outstanding is the value you bring to the board of life. There could be people who might have the same qualities as you, but you are still unique. You were created for such a time as this; there is something special about you.

Do you have the tenacity to pursue your passion which can bring great meaning to your life and to this world? Your value goes beyond just supporting you; it can support others too. Not chasing after your passion or dream is like winning a lotto ticket and refusing to cash it in.

What would have happened if Bill Gates decided to quit his pursuit of Microsoft, Steve Jobs with Apple, Mandela fighting apartheid, Madam Theresa, Kwame Nkrumah for Ghana's independence, Charles Wesley for most of our powerful hymns, or Zuckerberg for his innovative Facebook platform, which has connected people all over the globe? All these people, just to mention a few, devoted most of their time studying, practicing, and perfecting what they love.

I once watched in an interview where Michael Jackson was saying he practices about eight hours a day perfecting his dancing. Michael Jordan used to train hours perfecting his basketball shots. It's important to redirect your time and energy to things that you love; by doing so, you are adding value to yourself. Anything that is not valuable is destroyed, but things of value are protected and held in high esteem. God gave us His son Jesus because He valued Him and also valued us.

If you want to have more, you need to become more. People pay for value and not the time we put into the work. Value can be created and maintained by staying current. I had a close friend who was a mechanic, but he is no longer working as a mechanic because he was not able to go to school to learn the new technology used in modern, sophisticated cars. If you are an architect, you should know that people don't draw with pencils anymore. A lot has changed in almost every industry or vocation.

Most designs are done with computer software. Blockbuster movie center was very popular years back. I used to rent movies from a local store. They are no longer in business today. In my opinion, they did not keep up with the current trend of technology. Companies like Netflix put them out of business.

Blockbuster could have dedicated time and effort to finding out about how to move the business into the future. But they didn't. Years ago, people never ordered items without physically seeing it, touching it, or wearing it to see how it fit or looked like. Today, many people order online, which is causing many stores to close and concentrate on their web platform.

Zig Ziglar said: "Learn to work harder on yourself than your job. If you work hard on your job, you make a living, but if you work hard on yourself, you make a fortune." Try to always make yourself more valuable.

Also, understand that it's not what happens to you but what you do with what happens to you. The wind that destroys the trees is the same wind that makes the eagles soar high.

Let's look at the famine that Isaac encountered and the outcome in the book of Genesis:

> *[1] And there was a famine in the land, beside the first famine that was in the days of Abraham. And Isaac went unto Abimelech king of the Philistines unto Gerar. [2] And the LORD appeared unto him, and said, Go not down into Egypt; dwell in the land which I shall tell thee of: [3] Sojourn in this land, and I will be with thee, and will bless thee; for unto thee, and unto thy seed, I will give all these countries, and I will perform the oath which I swore unto Abraham, thy father; [4] And I will make thy seed to multiply as the stars of heaven, and will give unto thy seed all these countries; and in*

thy seed shall all the nations of the earth be blessed; *⁵Because*
that Abraham obeyed my voice and kept my charge, my
commandments, my statutes, and my laws.

¹²Then Isaac sowed in that land, and received in the same
year a hundredfold: and the LORD blessed him. 13 And
the man waxed great, and went forward, and grew until he
became very great: ¹⁴For he had possession of flocks and
possession of herds, and great store of servants: and the
Philistines envied him.

Genesis 26:1-5; 12-14 (ESV)

In the year when there was a great famine in the land of the
Philistines, and many people were leaving to Egypt, Isaac
inquired of the Lord, and he was instructed to stay and not
leave. When he obeyed God, his harvest was huge and even
scared the Philistines.

There are a few things that I want to mention here: The Bible
says in the book of Proverbs Chapter 3: 5-6 *"Trust in the LORD*
with all thine heart, and lean not unto thine own understanding. In all
thy ways acknowledge Him, and He shall direct thy paths."

Isaac trusted in the Lord and also listened to the Lord's
instructions by deciding to stay. God directed him to an
irrigation system that his father Abraham used, which was the
digging of wells. These wells were his secret to his bountiful
harvest. When studying these scriptures, the Lord revealed to
me that, investing in water and buying stocks in this area will
always be a long-lasting commodity because every living thing
on this earth will need water as long as they have life.

Isaac saw a need and created a solution, which created wealth. During the financial meltdown, Wall Street got the greatest hit, and many investors lost money as a result. However, many people made a lot of money because they bought stocks and real estate at a cheaper price and sold it when the market became better for huge profits.

It's always what you do in any situation that matters. It rained at the same location with two salespeople. One of them said, "Oh, what a storm. With a storm like this, who will make a sale; no one will come out." The other salesperson said, "With a storm like this, everyone will be home; what a day to make a great sale." It's your mindset and understanding the seasons and times.

Problems we solve can raise our value. The value of David was increased as soon as he killed Goliath. Goliath was the passport for David to become king. Esther solved the problem of massive genocide. The first computer that was created was about the size of a room. Steve Jobs solved a problem by making it small. Apple Inc. was started in his dad's garage.

A man's gift maketh room for him and bringeth him before great men.

Proverbs 18:16 (KJV)

Is there a unique gift that you have been able to identify? Every gift that the Creator placed in you is to bring you to your divine calling, potential, and fulfillment. Your ability to fulfill this assignment has already been prepared by God for you. Proverbs 18:16 states: "Your gift will bring you before great men." In using your gift, God will connect you with mentors or businessmen and investors. This is what I call divine helpers.

Myles Monroe says: "A gift cannot be learned; it can only be refined." A college cannot give you a gift. That's why people go to college for four years and are still broke because they are not refining the gift God gave to them.

One of the TV shows I always watch with my daughters is Shark Tank. I have seen many ideas on the show, and I always ask myself: I thought of this before; why didn't I start it?

One unique quality of most successful people is the **speed of implementation** of their ideas, dreams, and goals—and the ability to take action when you feel uncertain.

Prayer: *Heavenly Father, thank You for revealing to us that we are created to be successful. I know Your thoughts for us are good and will bring us to an expected end. We surrender our lives to You, Lord Jesus. Please reveal to us our gift and show us the problem we were born to solve. Amen.*

CHAPTER 3
BUILDING RELATIONSHIPS

I've learned that people will forget what you said, people will forget what you did, but people will never forget how you made them feel.

Maya Angelou

This is one of my favorite quotes of all time. I walk by this statement often, and therefore, it always reflects in how I treat first-time visitors at my church, my patients, my family, and everyone I come across.

As long as we live, we are always going to be dealing with people.

> **A healthy relationship in every sphere of our lives can be an ongoing spring of support and happiness in life.**

This spring can water our physical, spiritual, and mental wellbeing. An unhealthy relationship can drain us emotionally.

Van Moody said: *"People are like an elevator, the right people will take you up, and the wrong people will bring you down."*

Conflicts, divorce, broken homes and families, broken friendships, broken businesses, church splits or divisions, people walking out of churches, betrayals, and mistrusts are all connected to relationships.

Every relationship is built on simple principles: working hard on it, commitment, and a willingness to adapt and change with the people you're involved with.

> *Walk with the wise and become wise, for a companion of fools suffers harm.*
>
> Proverbs 13:20 (NIV)

With the inception of the mass social media frenzy, people associate great status with how many followers they have. Having many social followers does not mean you are loved. You can't be friends with everyone.

After God created the universe, He said: "Let us make man in our own image." There was the Trinity, and there was fellowship. After man was created, God enjoyed fellowshipping with the man that He created in His own image and likeness; no wonder we all naturally crave friendship and positive interactions.

> *And they heard the sound of the LORD God walking in the*
> *garden in the cool of the day...*
>
> Genesis 3:8 (KJV)

God will come daily to fellowship with man. The Bible never said that God had the same relationship with the angels. It's, therefore, very imperative that we work on creating healthy relationships. A good relationship gives to each other and does not become a parasite.

Understanding your worth and value is very significant when trying to get into any relationship. You can't add value to someone when you don't even value your own self.

> *Do not be misled: 'Bad company corrupts good character.'*
>
> 1 Corinthians 15:33 (NIV)

> *One who has unreliable friends soon comes to ruin, but there*
> *is a friend who sticks closer than a brother.*
>
> Proverbs 18:24 (NIV)

What kind of people do you walk, sit, or stand with? Do you pursue and identify with people of purpose? Are you selective when it comes to choosing friends? Do you seek divine directions, or do you just pick and choose anyone at all?

> *¹Blessed is the man that walketh not in the counsel of the ungodly, nor standeth in the way of sinners, nor sitteth in the seat of the scornful. ²But his delight is in the law of the LORD; and in his law doth he meditate day and night. ³And he shall be like a tree planted by the rivers of water, that bringeth forth his fruit in his season; his leaf also shall not wither; and whatsoever he doeth shall prosper. ⁴The ungodly are not so: but are like the chaff which the wind driveth away. ⁵Therefore the ungodly shall not stand in the judgment, nor sinners in the congregation of the righteous. ⁶For the LORD knoweth the way of the righteous: but the way of the ungodly shall perish.*
>
> Psalm 1:1-6 (KJV)

Psalm 1:1-6 outlines the qualities of a blessed man; it's very essential to walk with people who will add value to your life.

Let's look at some of the characteristics that help build healthy relationships by first observing the friendship between Jonathan and David.

SIX QUALITIES OF THE RELATIONSHIP BETWEEN JONATHAN AND DAVID

1. Jonathan and David had a strong bond. After

David killed Goliath and moved to Saul's palace, the Bible says "the soul of Jonathan was knit to the soul of David" (1 Sam. 18:1). They had a strong connection with each other. Certain friends that are even closer than siblings. I believe God can knit people together for a reason and a season.

2. Jonathan showed strong brotherly love. It will take an intense sacrificial love to risk your life, reputation, and rain of insults to stand or support someone you love during a crisis or for the person to fulfill their goal. Jonathan did the same for David, an immeasurable love. "Greater love has no one than this: to lay down one's life for one's friends" (John 15:13).

3. Genuine friends don't leave you in difficult times but always provide encouragement. When David was fleeing from Saul in the wilderness, Jonathan traveled to Horesh to support his friend (1 Sam. 23:16). God will always bring someone in your life during stormy days to encourage you. Do not forget the people God sends in your life to strengthen you in times of crisis.

4. Jonathan offered protection for his friend David. Jonathan realized his father was plotting to kill David. He did not support his father but warned David of the danger and also formulated a plan to provide a way of escape for his friend David (1 Sam. 19:1-4). Friends always protect, correct, and seek the success of their friends. Good friends always

speak the truth; sometimes the friend who has been advised might perceive it wrongly, but if you know you're listening to the voice of the Holy Spirit, keep on. Some people who will stick with their family, even if they know what they're doing is very wrong. Jonathan did not do that. Let's always stand for the truth, and God will bless us.

5. David trusted his friend Jonathan and confided and shared his pain with him. David said to Jonathan: "What have I done? What is my iniquity?" (1 Sam. 20:1). Jonathan kept all of David's frustrations a secret in his heart and was always figuring out a way to help him. There are friends that will always be there for you. They give you a shoulder to lean on when you are weak or going through trying moments. Those are true friends. Never forget their investments.

6. Jonathan is an unbelievable human being; I admire and love him so much. I pray for people like this in my life all the time. They are hard to come by. It was clear that David would become king of Israel one day, but Jonathan never harbored any jealousy in his heart. This would have actually been Jonathan's inheritance since he was Saul's son, but he acknowledged that God had chosen David instead. This is deep.

It was obvious that Jonathan had great self-esteem, self-worth, and valued himself. He was not intimidated by David at all. He believed that God had placed something unique in him (1

Sam. 18:3-4). A good friend will always want to see his friend success and celebrate their breakthrough. I thank God that in my life I can always celebrate my friends and cheer them on the path to their destiny. Jealousy destroys friendships. Always know that once you make it happen for others, God will make sure you get a greater portion. Don't close opportunities for others.

TRUST

Trust is defined as the reliance on the integrity, strength, ability, surety, etc., of a person or a thing. Trust is the foundation of every good relationship. We all trust some people in our lives: family, friends, church folks, managers, politicians, church leaders, national security, our military, and more. One thing these people may have in common is the ability for them to fail or betray our trust. Have you ever experienced a shattered trust or confidence? It can be very painful. Feeling hurt can lead to mistrust, which can become a seed that grows into a huge forest of bitterness. Trust take years to build, seconds to destroy, and forever to repair—so guard your trust. For it's one of the key pillars in any business venture. **When someone gives you their trust, they are telling you they are safe with you.** Appreciate that.

RESPECT

Respect is an important way of being kind and good to other people. Respect means thinking of how somebody else feels. Respect is treating another person the same way you'd want to be treated yourself! When you respect people, you value their input and ideas, and they value yours.

MINDFULNESS

It is important to be sensitive to people and be responsible for your words and actions. **Do unto others as you would want them to do unto you.**

COMMUNICATION

Lack of communication has been one of the most common causes for most business, personal, and relational problems that we encounter.

Communication is the process of transferring signals or messages between a sender and receiver through various methods (written words, nonverbal cues, spoken words). Relationships can be strongly enhanced through effective communication with those around you.

WHAT YOU CAN DO TO BUILD BETTER RELATIONSHIPS

1. Develop your people skills.

2. What relationship need do you have? And what do they need from you? Prove to people who are ready to deposit in you that you are ready to receive; do whatever they ask you to do; be accountable to and value their investment. Whenever you show intense interest in your

mentor or teacher, it becomes apparent to them you are worth their time and energy. I like an illustration that Van Moody gave, he said: "You need to prove that you are a fridge and not a trash receptor." A fridge preserves: are you ready to value, use, and preserve the information that you will be given? A trash bin just keeps waste and does not create any value. Mentors always want to invest in the refrigerators.

3. **Gratitude and Appreciation** will always make people give you 110%. In any organization, in any type of relationship, complimenting each other helps bring out the best in anyone. Don't forget about people who have made a great impact in your life. There was something special about Paul and his writings; he showed a lot of gratitude and thanksgiving. He always expressed how he felt in his letters. Never forget people who have been there for you. Gratitude will scale up your altitude and always makes people want to do more for you. Let's look at some of Paul's letters in the book of Romans 16:3-16 (NIV).

³Greet Priscilla and Aquila, my coworkers in Christ Jesus. ⁴They risked their lives for me. Not only I but all the churches of the Gentiles are grateful to them. ⁵Greet also the church that meets at their house. Greet my dear friend Epenetus, who was the first convert to Christ in the province of Asia. ⁶Greet Mary, who worked very hard for you. ⁷Greet Andronicus

*and Junia, my fellow Jews who have been in prison with me.
They are outstanding amon] the apostles, and they were in
Christ before I was. ⁸Greet Ampliatus, my dear friend in
the Lord. ⁹Greet Urbanus, our co-worker in Christ, and my
dear friend Stachys. ¹⁰Greet Apelles, whose fidelity to Christ
has stood the test. Greet those who belong to the household of
Aristobulus. ¹¹Greet Herodion, my fellow Jew. Greet those
in the household of Narcissus who are in the Lord. ¹²Greet
Tryphena and Tryphosa, those women who work hard in
the Lord. Greet my dear friend Persis, another woman who
has worked very hard in the Lord. ¹³Greet Rufus, chosen in
the Lord, and his mother, who has been a mother to me, too.
¹⁴Greet Asyncritus, Phlegon, Hermes, Patrobas, Hermas and
the other brothers and sisters with them. ¹⁵Greet Philologus,
Julia, Nereus and his sister, and Olympas and all the Lord's
people who are with them. ¹⁶Greet one another with a holy
kiss.*

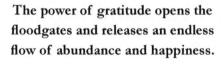

**The power of gratitude opens the
floodgates and releases an endless
flow of abundance and happiness.**

Always let people know how much you appreciate them; I
keep a gratitude diary, and it always works for me. Every now
and then, I will send greetings to every contact on my phone
list, send greeting cards during the holiday seasons, and make
phone calls: the responses are awesome and priceless.

4. **The power of being positive:** As a man
   thinks in his heart, so is he. Being positive is

attractive and contagious. People don't want to be around negative individuals all the time. The Law of Attraction teaches that just about anybody can attract whatever they desire if they can create it in their mind's eye and have an unfailing passion to see it manifest. Like Caleb, if you speak positivity and words that will build and motivate, you will inspire and push to recover all. This will spice up your relationship and see many doors opened for you.

5. **Active listening:** This is a beautiful gift that many people do not possess, and if you possess this attribute, you will attract many people. People respond very well to those who truly want to listen to what they have to say. It also shows that the person speaking to you is important.

RELATIONSHIP PRUNING

As you journey through this life, there will be people who will be with you from A-Z, others will only be with you from A-G, and still others from G-Z. Don't be afraid to cut off certain relationships that are not healthy. If God brings them into your life, He will connect you with other people for your next season.

Getting out of any relationship usually raises brows from people. Regardless of how the relationship changed or ended, be careful how you respond. Don't be very negative or speak very bad about it. I would suggest you respond like: "God is moving me to a different level or different calling." They may have been very supportive in your life, but you have to move on. Keep it plain and simple because all things happen for a reason.

Sometimes the issues we have in our relationship or friendship do not stem from the immediate core individual, but the weeds around the tree. Let's look at this scripture in Luke 13:6-9 (NIV):

> *⁶A man had a fig tree growing in his vineyard, and he went to look for fruit on it but did not find any. ⁷So, he said to the man who took care of the vineyard, 'For three years now I've been coming to look for fruit on this fig tree and haven't found any. Cut it down! Why should it use up the soil?' ⁸'Sir,' the man replied, 'leave it alone for one more year, and I'll dig around it and fertilize it. 9If it bears fruit next year, fine! If not, then cut it down.'*

The man dug around the fig tree. The digging around, pruning, and cutting weeds out is descriptive of how we're supposed to treat our parents, friends, family members, or cheerleaders. Sometimes you have to cut some of these people off if you know they are not promoting your relationship. The fertilizer (dung/mess) that He puts around the tree is to enable the tree to grow very beautifully. Everything will work together for your good.

The mess (dung) is the difficult times that we go through as believers; they always make us strong and prepare us to handle fruitfulness at the next level.

SOME SIGNS THAT SHOWS PRUNING IS OVER

A sign that shows that the relationship is coming to an end is when an individual can't accept a change of status in your life. Some people will be OK with you as long as you rely on them for everything. Some people cannot celebrate the blessings of God in your life.

> **If they can't be happy for your elevation, it will be difficult for them to celebrate your destination.**

Loyalty is a key ingredient in every relationship. If a friend can't be faithful during your moment of crisis, then they need to go. You need to stick with people who are ready to stand by you through thick and thin and don't forget their sacrifices. There are groups of people that are fake supporters. In private settings, they show their love and allegiance to you, but in public, they turn away and won't defend you.

SEASONS AND STAGES IN EVERY RELATIONSHIP

Let's look at 2 Kings 2:1-6 (KJV)

[1] And it came to pass, when the Lord would take up Elijah into heaven by a whirlwind, that Elijah went with Elisha from Gilgal.

[2] And Elijah said unto Elisha, Tarry here, I pray thee; for the Lord hath sent me to Bethel. And Elisha said unto him, As the Lord liveth, and as thy soul liveth, I will not leave thee. So they went down to Bethel.

[3] And the sons of the prophets that were at Bethel came forth to Elisha, and said unto him, Knowest thou that the Lord will take away thy master from thy head to day? And he said, Yea, I know it; hold ye your peace.

[4] And Elijah said unto him, Elisha, tarry here, I pray thee; for the Lord hath sent me to Jericho. And he said, As the Lord liveth, and as thy soul liveth, I will not leave thee. So they came to Jericho.

[5] And the sons of the prophets that were at Jericho came to Elisha, and said unto him, Knowest thou that the Lord will take away thy master from thy head to day? And he answered, Yea, I know it; hold ye your peace.

[6] And Elijah said unto him, Tarry, I pray thee, here; for the Lord hath sent me to Jordan. And he said, As the Lord liveth, and as thy soul liveth, I will not leave thee. And they two went on.

For any relationship to be healthy and strong, there will be places where we will inevitably visit. Elijah and Elisha went through these places, which included Gilgal, Bethel, Jericho, and Jordan. These places have a lot of precious truth that we can glean from.

How did **Gilgal** come about?

Joshua 5:2, 5-9 (NIV)

> *²At that time the Lord said to Joshua, 'Make flint knives and circumcise the Israelites again.'*
>
> *⁵All the people that came out had been circumcised, but all the people born in the wilderness during the journey from Egypt had not.*
> *⁶The Israelites had moved about in the wilderness forty years until all the men who were of military age when they left Egypt had died, since they had not obeyed the Lord. For the Lord had sworn to them that they would not see the land he had solemnly promised their ancestors to give us, a land flowing with milk and honey.*
> *⁷So he raised up their sons in their place, and these were the ones Joshua circumcised. They were still uncircumcised because they had not been circumcised on the way.*
> *⁸And after the whole nation had been circumcised, they remained where they were in camp until they were healed.*
> *⁹Then the Lord said to Joshua, 'Today I have rolled away the reproach of Egypt from you.' So, the place has been called Gilgal to this day.*

Gilgal is the cutting place (make flint knives and circumcise), also meaning the blade of truth. *For the word of God is alive and active. Sharper than any double-edged sword, it penetrates even to dividing soul and spirit, joints and marrow; it judges the thoughts and attitudes of the heart* (Hebrews 4:12 NIV).

This means those in the relationship need to speak the truth without reservation and say things as they are. If someone is on the wrong path, you should be able to bring it to their attention. In most cases, people want to hear what makes them feel good.

Good advice is a powerful tool to bring one to their destination. Depending and feeding off the people you have surrounded yourself with will make your journey to success less stressful. **Your journey to success will be less stressful depending on the people you surround yourself with.**

For whom the Lord loves He chastens, and scourges every son whom He receives.

Hebrews 12:6 (KJV)

David was rebuked by Nathan, and he accepted the correction in good faith.

BETHEL

[16]Then Jacob awoke from his sleep and said, 'Surely the Lord is in this place, and I did not know it.'
[17]And he was afraid and said, 'How awesome is this place! This is none other than the house of God, and this is the gate of heaven!'
[18]Then Jacob rose early in the morning, and took the stone that he had put at his head, set it up as a pillar, and poured oil on top of it.
[19]And he called the name of that place Bethel; but the name of that city had been Luz previously.

Genesis 28:16-19 (ESV)

Bethel symbolizes the presence of God. Elijah and Elisha went there to pray and worship. Praying together builds strong bonds, creates harmony, and keeps the devil away. The house of God is a place of revelation because God's presence resides in our midst when we gather. God's place is a very fertile place: the birthplace of visions and dreams and of healing and restoration.

JERICHO

13Now when Joshua was near Jericho, he looked up and saw a man standing in front of him with a drawn sword in his hand. Joshua went up to him and asked, 'Are you for us or for our enemies?'

14'Neither,' he replied, 'but as commander of the army of the Lord I have now come.' Then Joshua fell facedown to the ground in reverence, and asked him, 'What message does my Lord have for his servant?'

15The commander of the Lord's army replied, 'Take off your sandals, for the place where you are standing is holy.' And Joshua did so.

Joshua 5:13-15 (NIV)

Jericho is known to have fortified walls. Elijah and Elisha came to this place. People mostly stay behind walls hiding their feelings and pain. Two cannot walk together unless they agree and are open to each other. Be open to showing your wounds or scars so that the binding of wounds can begin and for healing to take place. People hide their hearts and pain until it explodes. Have you ever had a friend who would never express how they feel when you offend them? They would try to wait and hold it in, and then one day, pour out all their fury on you. This drains you emotionally and psychologically.

"When Joshua was by Jericho," the scripture says, "he looked up and saw a man standing before him with a drawn sword in his hand." He was by Jericho but moved his eyes off the walls, looked up, and saw a man. There was a wall preventing Joshua and his team from taking over the territory. In any relationship, you will come to a point where you find yourself in Jericho behind those walls (the walls are any challenges that we face in a relationship). Ultimately, **whatever gets your attention, gets you** and has a way of consuming you. The more you think about it and focus on it, the bigger it gets; the more overwhelming it appears, the more it weighs you down. I have been there before.

But now notice Joshua "looked up and saw." That means he turned his eyes and his attention away from Jericho. And if he hadn't done that, Jericho wouldn't have fallen. Turning their eyes and attention away means they now want to talk about the issue, which has previously been hidden. They want to open up about their hurt, letting go, and leaving it all to God. When you are seeking help, make sure you go to those you trust and those who can understand where you are.

JORDAN

This is the final place Elijah and Elisha visited before Elijah was taken to heaven. Jordan symbolized a new beginning or transition. After letting go in Jericho, God will begin to renew every aspect of your life. A new unction, a new relationship, a fresh start, a new purpose, and a new vision—healed from every pain and hurt because every level of promotion comes with its own challenges. God always prepares us but also finds out if He can trust us with His favor.

Let's look at a couple of people who went through some form of transition at Jordan.

Naaman was healed of his leprosy by washing himself seven times in the Jordan according to the command of Elisha (2 Kings 5:1-14).

JOSHUA'S TRANSITION AT THE JORDAN RIVER

For Joshua, crossing the Jordan River meant entering the Promised Land and leaving the leadership of Moses.

> *For the LORD your God dried up the waters of the Jordan for you until you passed over, as LORD your God did to the Red Sea, which He dried up for us until we had passed over.*
> Joshua 4:23 (ESV)

Joshua connected their powerful redemption as a nation to the same power of God that helped them enter the Promised Land. They erected stones to commemorate the event.

ELISHA'S TRANSITION

Another significant transition occurred in the same location at Jordan when Elijah transferred the prophetic mantle to Elisha just before Elijah ascended to heaven. Elijah and Elisha walked on dry land through the Jordan River (2 Kings 2:8), just as Joshua had. At the Jordan, a new era began for Elisha.

JESUS'S TRANSITION

John the Baptist chose this same area to baptize because the Jordan River represented a place of transition—in fact, of new beginnings—it became the place where John baptized Jesus, preparing Him for the beginning of His ministry. But instead of the waters parting, the heavens did (Mark 1:10).

PART-TIME AND FULL-TIME FRIENDS

[11]But Naomi said, 'Return home, my daughters. Why would you come with me? Am I going to have any more sons, who could become your husbands?
[12]Return home, my daughters; I am too old to have another husband. Even if I thought there was still hope for me—even if I had a husband tonight and then gave birth to sons—
[13]would you wait until they grew up? Would you remain unmarried for them? No, my daughters. It is more bitter for me than for you, because the Lord's hand has turned against me!'
[14]At this they wept aloud again. Then Orpah kissed her mother-in-law goodbye, but Ruth clung to her.
[15]'Look,' said Naomi, 'your sister-in-law is going back to her people and her gods. Go back with her.'

¹⁶But Ruth replied, 'Don't urge me to leave you or to turn back from you. Where you go I will go, and where you stay I will stay. Your people will be my people and your God my God.

¹⁷Where you die I will die, and there I will be buried. May the Lord deal with me, be it ever so severely, if even death separates you and me.'

¹⁸When Naomi realized that Ruth was determined to go with her, she stopped urging her.

Ruth 1:11-18 (NIV)

Tragedies sometimes help to find out our real friends; some friends will be with you full-time, others will be around part-time. Orpah turned, but Ruth stood by Naomi. Sometimes people will change when directions change. There are people whose love is so strong, you can never convince them to stop a good deed. Some people have regretted becoming like Ruth, but God is not unjust; don't give up because He will reward you.

> **When a Ruth comes your way, cherish them because they tend to be extremely loyal and will risk their own life for you.**

Another group of full-time friends is the four friends who brought their sick friend to Jesus.

¹A few days later, when Jesus again entered Capernaum, the

people heard that he had come home.
²They gathered in such large numbers that there was no room left, not even outside the door, and he preached the word to them.
³Some men came, bringing to him a paralyzed man, carried by four of them.
⁴Since they could not get him to Jesus because of the crowd, they made an opening in the roof above Jesus by digging through it and then lowered the mat the man was lying on.
⁵When Jesus saw their faith, he said to the paralyzed man, 'Son, your sins are forgiven.'

Mark 2:1-5 (NIV)

This paralyzed friend needed help to come to Jesus. His four friends could have given many excuses or just showed sympathy, but instead, they showed compassion (the love of God that puts people into action), faith, determination, and love. These friends had the power of a made-up mind or oneness. They were focused on making sure their friend was healed. They had faith in Jesus Christ, in spite of the crowd. They were determined to do whatever it takes to bring their friend to Jesus. To get what you are passionate about, you have to do the extraordinary.

> **The greatest expression of love is that love seeks the welfare of the unlovable and undeserving.**

Love will make you go above and beyond yourself. Paul said:

"Bear one another's burden, and so fulfill the law of Christ" (Gal. 6:2 ESV). Sometimes the burdens are our friends' problems, but at times, it seems like the burden is our friends themselves.

It is our Christian duty to help. What we can also learn from this story is the power of collaboration, teamwork, and networking. Collaboration isn't about being best friends, or even liking the people you work with, it is about putting your differences aside and focusing on the common goal.

This brings to mind what I recently learned called social capital, and I will share this briefly. The Organization for Economic Co-operation and Development (OECD) defined social capital as: "Networks together with shared norms, values, and understandings that facilitate co-operation within or among groups."

In this definition, we can think of networks as real-world links between groups or individuals. Think of networks of friends, family, former colleagues, and so on. Our shared norms, values, and understandings are less concrete than our social networks. Varieties of social capital include:

Bonds: Links to people based on a sense of common identity (people like us)—such as family, close friends, and people who share our culture or ethnicity.

Bridges: Links that stretch beyond a shared sense of identity, for example distant friends, colleagues, and associates.

Linkages: Links to people or groups further up or lower down the social ladder.

The potential benefits of social capital can be seen by looking at social bonds. Friends and family can help us in lots of ways—emotionally, socially, and economically. The most successful people will tell you about someone they met, a mentor, who led them through the ropes to where they are today.

I am always trying to gain that type of capital hugely. Join groups, attend events in the community, meet people, and always show you are interested in what they do; be in a position where they will love to pour out their knowledge to you.

I want to end this chapter with this piece:

I heard about this beautiful practice in Japan some time back. The day before hearing this piece, I had stayed up all night working on this book, and there is a chapter where I write about challenges that we go through which prepare us for God's promotion. So, when I heard about this practice and how I understood it, it filled my heart with great joy and elevated my spirit to a different level.

I am very much particular about what I feed myself with in the morning, starting my day after my daily quiet time. Understanding that any pain, suffering, or breakdown we go through will all work together for our good. When you are down, the only other way is to get up. A lot of sports start by bending or kneeling, so when you are down, it means you are about to jump.

OK, so this is the story:

Whenever a bowl or anything ceramic breaks in Japan, it's put back together. The cracks are then filled—with GOLD, creating a beautiful lining. This is to emphasize the beauty in what was once broken. They believe that when something has suffered damage and has a history, it makes it more beautiful—and the same can be said for human beings.

Everything you're going through doesn't make your life uglier, although it may seem that way while going through it. It's up to you to choose to paint it with gold and make it beautiful or otherwise.

You are not broken beyond repair; you can pick yourself up and learn from what happened and become a better person because of it. Because of the struggles that you've been through, you can wear your scars proudly—as a badge of honor—as if to say: look at what I've been through. It's made me who I am today, and I can get through everything that life puts in front of me now.

My best moments, lessons, and achievements erupted from what I saw as shame, disappointment, and betrayal. The devil will mean it for evil, but God will turn it around for good.

People have become great entrepreneurs after they were fired or laid off from their job.

> **I believe God sometimes will stir things around in our comfort zone to get us to move on to new horizons.**

A young boy was bullied by friends that he had once served in difficult times past. They threw this boy into a pit and left him there. This boy was very scared, upset, and disappointed for what his friends had done to him. While in the pit, he saw a bag covered with leaves; to his surprise, the small bag was filled with gold coins. He gradually managed to come out of the pit.

Today, he is a multi-millionaire. His friends thought they were getting rid of him because they were threatened by him because of his intelligence—only later did they realize that they had just catapulted him to greatness.

Nobody has had a perfect life, and nobody will ever have. It's up to us if we choose to paint our broken pieces gold and make them beautiful. Don't be ashamed of what has happened to you; everything that has happened to you, happened for a reason.

We need to sit down and find what's useful in the struggle and how we can paint the cracks in our broken pieces with gold by turning something that could be ugly into something beautiful and inspiring.

> **When what you've been through
> becomes an inspiration to others, then
> you know it was all worth it.**

Don't get stuck on how things used to be. Every next level that God wants to take you will require different unction, strength, and ability, and sometimes, it takes being broken to achieve the qualities for the next level.

Thank you for reading up till this far; let's move to the next level and learn about entrepreneurship and investment.

CHAPTER 4
ENTREPRENEURSHIP

Entrepreneurship is simply defined as running your own business. It's a mindset, a way of thinking, and it's about picturing new ways to solve problems, which then create value. Qualities that entrepreneurs have are passion, relentlessness, and stamina that drives their actions. There is special energy that they possess, which enables them to push through and skip any hurdles.

An entrepreneur takes an idea—be it a product or service—then develops the needed skills, the courage, and the willingness to take the risk and do whatever it takes to turn the dream into a reality.

These are great tips for aspiring entrepreneurs from experts that will be very helpful:

One of the best ways to learn is through our mistakes

or failures. It's, therefore, just as significant to learn from businesses that fail as it is to study those that are successful.

> **Cultivating humility to learn from the mistakes of others before making them yourself is the secret to success.**

Other secrets include mentorship, reading books in the area you have chosen, networking, and self-development. The most successful people are always reading. The power that you possess is your knowledge. No one can take that from you.

Whatever you decide to do, make sure that is exactly what you, indeed, want to do. Entrepreneurship involves so much hard work. The key is persistence; most entrepreneurs fail many times before they finally find the right business or approach or strategy that made them successful.

The problem you are created to solve becomes your purpose. Finding solutions to the problem you identified then becomes the business. For example, you start working for a particular food cartel, but there aren't enough vendors to meet the high demand for food. That is a problem! You work at a hospital, but there is never enough transportation for patients on the day of discharge. That's another problem right there; what will the solution be?

Passion and persistence are every entrepreneur's fuel. Successful entrepreneurs are driven by the need for achievement and desire to make a difference.

WHY INCORPORATE?

A corporation is merely a file folder with some legal documents in it, sitting in some attorney's office registered with a state government agency. It's not a big building with a corporation name plastered on it. My first business, Royale Worldwide Corporation, was created in the State of Wyoming; it was sitting in a folder in my house until we established a sub-business, which was our first Home Care that started in an office space.

In the American system, and I believe in many other countries, being your own boss is the way to go. We are not taught in school how to be our own boss, but we are thought about how to be the best employees.

Whenever you ask someone if they've thought about starting their own business, they doubt themselves or their ability; but when they attend interviews for a job, they market themselves very well. There are great abilities in you; don't be afraid to start. **Life is made up of risks.** Your boss took a risk to create that job for you. Entrepreneurship is taking a calculated risk. The United States government is funded by tax dollars.

The best and easiest way is through payroll taxes. So, the government will partner with the entrepreneur and give them tax breaks. When that happens, you will hire more employees to grow your business. When more people are hired, there will be more payroll deductions from all the employees, which will then fund the government. The employer is an asset to the government.

The interesting part is the employee pays taxes first, before taking the rest home, while the employer pays taxes after their expenses. If an entrepreneur made one million dollars and can prove all his expenses, which include the healthcare expenses of the employees and all other business expenses in that year, and the total is $900,000.00, then the entrepreneur will only be taxed on the remaining $100,000.00.

What if you employ your son as an employee and set up a scholarship fund, which he can use to further his education, will that be a tax write off? If you give your daughter, who is also employed in the company, a company car, can that also be a tax write off? The government is not against the entrepreneur; they want the entrepreneur to be well off so that they can expand their business.

Robert Kiyosaki explained this topic very well in his book "Rich Dad, Poor Dad." He explains understanding the law. For instance, utilizing a corporation wrapped around the knowledge of accounting, investing, and markets can create great growth. One who has the knowledge in tax advantages and protection provided by a corporation can get rich so much faster than someone who is an employee or a small-business sole proprietor.

1. Tax advantage: A corporation pays for expenses before it pays taxes. Employees earn

and get taxed and then live on what is left. A corporation earns, spends everything it can, and is taxed on anything that is left. The rich take advantage of this legal tax loophole. For example, by owning your own corporation, you get to enjoy vacations, car payments, insurance, and repairs at the company's expense, but do it legally—with pre-tax dollars.

2. Protection from lawsuits: Our society is filled with litigations; everybody wants to sue somebody. The rich hide much of their wealth using mediums such as corporations and trusts to protect their assets.

I love this summary by Robert:

The Rich who own Corporations:

1. Earn
2. Spend
3. Pay taxes

People who work for Corporations:

1. Earn
2. Pay taxes
3. Spend

Pursuing wealth as a business owner or corporation is very important. Before we go on, let's look at the secret of the Jewish people.

*¹And if you faithfully obey the voice of the Lord your God,
being careful to do all His commandments that I command
you today, the Lord your God will set you high above all the
nations of the earth.*

*¹³And the Lord will make you the head and not the tail,
and you shall only go up and not down, if you obey the
commandments of the Lord your God, which I command you
today, being careful to do them.*

Deuteronomy 28:1, 13 (ESV)

*But ye are a chosen generation, a royal priesthood, a holy
nation, a peculiar people; that ye should show forth the
praises of him who hath called you out of darkness into his
marvelous light.*

1 Peter 2:9 (KJV)

As children of God, you have to believe that you are God's chosen generation, unique in His sight. Jewish people believe these scriptures so much that it drives them to succeed. We should also have these beliefs engraved in our minds and hearts and pass it on to our children and our children's children too.

According to the Forbes 2016 report of the wealthiest Jews in the world, Zuckerberg added $11.2 billion to his net wealth, giving him a total fortune of $44.6 billion and moving him up to No. 6 on the list from No. 16 in the previous year. The surge sends the Facebook founder past last year's richest Jew, Oracle CEO Larry Ellison, and runner-up, former New York City Mayor Michael Bloomberg.

Ellison is seventh on the list, with a net worth of $43.6 billion, followed by Bloomberg, with $40 billion. Ellison's net worth dropped over $10 billion, from $54.2 billion last year, while Bloomberg's wealth increased from about $35.5 billion.

Zuckerberg, who is still one of the youngest billionaires, announced last December that he and his wife, Priscilla Chan, will donate 99 percent of their shares in the social media company over the course of their lifetimes.

Google co-founders Larry Page and Sergey Brin are Nos. 12 and 13 on the Forbes list, with $35.2 billion and $34.4 billion, respectively.

Sheldon Adelson, the casino magnate and influential Republican donor, saw his wealth drop to $25.2 billion from $31.4 billion last year, falling to No. 22 on the list.

Hedge fund manager George Soros ($24.9 billion), Dell founder and CEO Michael Dell ($19.8 billion), Brazilian-Jewish banker Joseph Safra ($17.2 billion), investor Carl Icahn ($17 billion) and hedge fund manager James Simons ($15.5 billion) are the other Jews in the top 50.

While far less numerous than their male counterparts, there are a number of Jewish women billionaires. On the list are Shari Arison ($3.9 billion), Pritzker family scion Karen Pritzker ($3.8 billion), Lynn Schusterman ($3.4 billion), Joan Tisch ($3.3 billion), and Gap co-founder Doris Fisher ($2.6 billion).

Sheryl Sandberg also makes the cut with a net worth of $1.2 billion. The influential Facebook COO and "Lean In" author donated about $31 million of Facebook stock to multiple charities.

The non-Jewish Bill Gates remains at the top of the list—where he has been for the past three years and 17 of the past 22—with a net worth of $75 billion.

Forbes found 1,810 billionaires worldwide, down from the 1,826 a year ago.

H.W. Charles explained hidden truths about the Jewish people that we can all learn. Men such as Abraham, Isaac, Jacob, and Solomon—who followed God diligently—walked in divine prosperity. Jews believe the blessing of wealth is dependent on obedience to the law and covenant.

You attract what you think about. What is your view about money? Do you think it's as evil as some people perceive it to be? When you love it more than anything else, then it becomes evil. When you depend on money solely and not God, then it becomes a god unto you.

In the book of Matthew 19:16, 21-22 (KJV) there is an interesting conversation between Jesus and a rich, young man.

> *[16] And, behold, one came and said unto him, 'Good Master, what good thing shall I do, that I may have eternal life?'*

²¹Jesus said unto him, 'If thou wilt be perfect, go and sell that thou hast, and give to the poor, and thou shalt have treasure in heaven: and come and follow me.'
²²But when the young man heard that saying, he went away sorrowful: for he had great possessions.

This young rich man had followed the Ten Commandments as a little boy, but when Jesus asked him to sell his possessions and give the proceeds to the poor, he could not do what Jesus asked him to do because he was very attached to his material possessions.

I believe the lack of money also makes people do things they wouldn't otherwise do. Poverty has led people into prostitution, the drug trade, violence, murder, black magic (sakawa), and so much more.

A feast is made for laughter, and wine maketh merry: but money answereth all things.
Ecclesiastes 10:19 (KJV)

Many people quote this scripture: you cannot serve God and Mammon (Luke 16:13). The serving of Mammon is when people work their whole life for money, instead of working for some years and allowing their money to work for them.

GO TO THE ANT

Consider Proverbs 6:6-11 (ESV)

⁶Go to the ant, O sluggard;
consider her ways, and be wise.
⁷Without having any chief,
officer, or ruler,
⁸she prepares her bread in summer
and gathers her food in harvest.
⁹How long will you lie there, O sluggard?
When will you arise from your sleep?
¹⁰A little sleep, a little slumber,
a little folding of the hands to rest,
¹¹and poverty will come upon you like a robber,
and want like an armed man.

When I was a little boy, I used to marvel at how ants carry bread crumbs and travel in a line into a hole. I thought they were just carrying the food to eat it. I had no idea the biblical revelation until my grandpa told me: "They are storing all that food for the rainy season where they will not be able to come out for food. That's their survival diet." As a little boy, I was so fascinated about how this tiny insect could be that smart.

Verse 10 admonishes us to work very hard and not to slack. H. W. Charles advises that the key is to work extremely hard for a certain period of time (1-10 years), create abundant wealth, and then make your money work hard for you through wise investments that yield passive income for life. Many business owners work very hard the first few years of their business, 24/7. Once the business is prospering, they then sell it for a high profit and then move on to other ventures that produce even more revenue.

Those who work their land will have abundant food, but those
who chase fantasies will have their fill of poverty.

Proverbs 28:19 (NIV)

Jews understand that they must work in a high-paying career
or own their business and not sit down depending on God for
a living, but as they work, Jehovah God will bless their handy
work. We will look at some investments in the last chapter.

God wants to bless us so that we will be a blessing unto others.
Jews don't see wealth as evil because they believe it's from
God. The question is why should God bless me? Jews value
wealth for the sake of caring for their families and helping the
needy. Unlike some Christians who view poverty as virtuous,
Jews view poverty negatively. Like Jews, we need to understand
that there is nothing we have that we were not given.

> **As we become wealthy, we should
> never forget to give God the glory
> because He is the one who showered
> us with those blessings.**

Look at this scripture in the book of Deuteronomy 8:11-19
(ESV):

*[11]Take care lest you forget the Lord your God by not keeping
his commandments and his rules and his statutes, which I
command you today,*
[12]lest, when you have eaten and are full and have built good

houses and live in them,

¹³and when your herds and flocks multiply and your silver and gold is multiplied and all that you have is multiplied,

¹⁴then your heart be lifted up, and you forget the Lord your God, who brought you out of the land of Egypt, out of the house of slavery,

¹⁵who led you through the great and terrifying wilderness, with its fiery serpents and scorpions and thirsty ground where there was no water, who brought you water out of the flinty rock,

¹⁶who fed you in the wilderness with manna that your fathers did not know, that he might humble you and test you, to do you good in the end.

¹⁷Beware lest you say in your heart, 'My power and the might of my hand have gotten me this wealth.'

¹⁸You shall remember the Lord your God, for it is he who gives you power to get wealth, that he may confirm his covenant that he swore to your fathers, as it is this day.

¹⁹And if you forget the Lord your God and go after other gods and serve them and worship them, I solemnly warn you today that you shall surely perish.

The majority of Jews are business owners; they are mostly employers instead of employees. You can find a great number of them as product inventors or in real estate development, publishing industries, the hospitality business, or entertainment industries. Look at some of the Jewish-owned businesses: Google, Facebook, Wikipedia, eBay, Microsoft, Dell, Goldman Sachs, New York Times, Sears, Starbucks, Columbia Pictures, Fox, Disney, CBS, HBO. These businesses were created, and I believe you and I can do it too.

When God created Adam in His image and likeness, He placed creative abilities in man to also create things, not just to consume them. God created the trees in the garden, and from that, man created the beautiful furniture we see and use around us.

One of God's purposes is to perfect His creation through innovations.

> **Every problem we have, or anything that we are not happy about, we have the capacity to change.**

By changing it, we can create a business. There will be many obstacles on the way, but perseverance, which is the continuous persistence in a course of action in spite of difficulties or discouragement, will take us to the land of great achievements.

May God open the eyes of our understanding to see clearly all the abilities He has placed in us.

Whoever loves pleasure will become poor; whoever loves wine and olive oil will never be rich.

Proverbs 21:17 (NIV)

Those who concentrate on luxury and buying beyond their means cannot be rich. It's good to build credit, but don't buy what you can't afford. Some people are working very hard to pay for huge credit card bills because they made purchases way above their means. As we journey to the land of wealth, we need to hold back on spending and save as much as we can, even if it means living prudently. Joseph's popularity in Egypt was based on the directions he received from God to save for the future.

> *A good man leaves an inheritance to his children's children,*
> *but the sinner's wealth is laid up for the righteous.*
> Proverbs 13:22 (ESV)

I am working to leave an inheritance for my children's children, and I pray you will do that too. To leave an inheritance, you have to work hard, save, and preserve what you have worked for—for your children.

> *Invest in seven ventures, yes, in eight, you do not know what*
> *disaster may come on the land.*
> Ecclesiastes 11:2 (NIV)

Invest in different types of investments. If you can, invest in seven or eight different types. There will be a sample list in the investment chapter that will be very helpful to you.

Jews do not play around with their laws and covenants.

> *I will also bless the foreigners who commit themselves to the*
> *LORD, who serve Him and love His name, who worship*
> *Him and do not desecrate the Sabbath day of rest, and who*
> *hold fast to my covenant.*
> Isaiah 56:6 (NLT)

This scripture makes me understand that you don't have to be a Jew to be blessed by God. Our financial blessing is tied to wisdom from the word of God. The word of God is divided into the Old and New Testament. Testament means "covenant" or "contract." It's a written agreement between two or more people.

Jews use what is called the Torah. The Torah contains agreements between God and his people. God makes promises to His people, and in return, He wants His people to do certain things or obey, serve, and love Him.

> *This Book of the Law shall not depart from your mouth, but you shall meditate on it day and night, so that you may be careful to do according to all that is written in it. For then you will make your way prosperous, and then you will have good success.*
>
> Joshua 1:8 (ESV)

Our prosperity is linked to studying God's word, which will also give us wisdom. If we do what it says, we will be successful. These are some of the books you will find in most Jewish homes. The Torah is very common, which means the Law, and is found in the Talmud; the rest are Mishnab, Tosefta, and Shulchan Aruch.

Tithing. Deuteronomy 14:22: Thou shalt surely tithe. Religious Jews are very particular about tithing. Maaser Kesafim means giving at least ten percent of their income to the poor. Jews believe their wealth is connected to their faithfulness in tithing. Some of the Jewish laws say: give tithes so that you will be prosperous (Asser te'asser – Shabbat 119a).

One of the famous statements made by John D. Rockefeller states: "I never would have been able to tithe the first million dollars I ever made if I had not tithed my first salary, which was $1.50 per week." One of the richest men in history tithed. I know there are many teachings about tithing. I believe in tithing, and it's been working for me. Without faith, it is impossible to please God. Tithing is done by faith.

> *Bring the full tithe into the storehouse, that there may be food in my house. And thereby put me to the test, says the Lord of hosts, if I will not open the windows of heaven for you and pour down for you a blessing until there is no more need. 11 I will rebuke the devourer for you, so that it will not destroy the fruits of your soil, and your vine in the field shall not fail to bear, says the Lord of hosts. 12 Then all nations will call you blessed, for you will be a land of delight, says the Lord of hosts.*
>
> Malachi 3: 10 (ESV)

May this be fulfilled in our lives and in the lives of our children's children in Jesus name.

GIVING

> *For there will never cease to be poor in the land. Therefore, I command you, 'You shall open wide your hand to your brother, to the needy and to the poor, in your land.'*

Give, and it will be given to you. A good measure, pressed
down, shaken together, and running over will be poured into
your lap. For with the measure you use, it will be measured
back to you.

Luke 6:38 (NIV)

I have read many books or followed many people who are
not even Christians that are always giving to charity or have
charity organizations that are always giving to the needy and
poor. I strongly believe that Luke 6:38 is a universal law, which
I believe will bless you regardless of your religious affiliation
when put into practice.

Look at the most successful people in the world who are always
giving to poor people all over the world: they keep getting rich.
The Bill Gates Foundation, Warren Buffett, Oprah Winfrey,
and Richard Branson, just to mention a few. Most Muslims
eventually make the journey to Mecca, and when they return,
they give lots of alms to the poor, and as a result, they enjoy
increase.

I have experienced this kind of blessings myself; the more I
give, the more I receive. Many philanthropists in this world
are always giving to the poor, and it's been working for them.
Always be in a position to help those in need. God will bless
you to be a blessing. Some people are not being blessed

because they do not have a vision that is in line with God's agenda. You can also volunteer at shelters, Red Cross, or any other organization that is involved with helping people in need. Whatever you can do, please do it. Gather clothes, shoes, books, hospital supplies, first aid kits, etc., and give them to poor villages across the world. In your own small way, you will greatly help someone in need. May God continue to direct your path.

CHAPTER 5
INVESTMENTS

*If you don't find a way to make money while you sleep, you
will work until you die.*

Warren Buffett

Investing is how you make your money grow, or appreciate,
for a long-term financial goal. It is a way of saving your money
for something further ahead in the future.

Investopedia defines investing as the act of committing money
or capital to an endeavor (a business, project, real estate, etc.)
with the expectation of obtaining additional income or profit.
Investing also can include the amount of time you put into
the study of a prospective company, especially since time is
money.

One question that changed my financial life was **if you don't
have a paycheck coming in, how will you survive?** It is

very important to have different streams of income.

Saving is a plan to set aside a certain amount of your earned income over a short period of time to be able to accomplish a short-term goal.

Malachi chapter three instructs us to bring a tenth of our income to the store house. We will use a farmer as the investor in this illustration. The Lord blesses the farmer with a bountiful harvest. He divides his harvest into ten, brings just one to the storehouse, and keeps the ninth portion. He also decides to give an additional portion as an offering. The farmer can also decide to eat the whole ninth portion or save one portion to re-plant (investment) for the next season. Because of his faithfulness, God will bless the seed he sows. Guess what? If he decides to eat all the harvested seeds, how will he have another harvest? God wants us to harvest, and we pray for God's divine wisdom to be able to invest in different portfolios to increase wealth. Our tithe protects our investment.

STOCKS

Stocks are literally certificates that say you own a portion of a company.

It doesn't matter how small your investment will be, at least you have started. Gradually, it will grow. Little drops of water make a mighty ocean.

And though your beginning was small, your latter days will be very great.

Job 8:7 (ESV)

Now let's discuss areas in which you can invest. Savings are the least type of investment. We can read about that in the story of the talents in Matthew 25:24-27 (ESV):

[24] He also who had received the one talent came forward, saying, 'Master, I knew you to be a hard man, reaping where you did not sow, and gathering where you scattered no seed, [25] So, I was afraid, and I went and hid your talent in the ground. Here, you have what is yours.' [26] But his master answered him, 'You wicked and slothful servant! You knew that I reap where I have not sown and gather where I scattered no seed? [27] Then you ought to have invested my money with the bankers, and at my coming I should have received what was my own with interest.'

The master was saying, worst case scenario, you should have kept my money in the bank; the small interest would have been better than nothing at all. Diversification is defined as a risk management technique that mixes a wide variety of investments within a portfolio. This management plan was in the Bible a long time ago. Ecclesiastes 11:2 says: "Give a portion to seven, or even to eight, for you know not what disaster may happen on earth." It's, therefore, important to invest in different type of businesses.

1. **High-Interest Savings Accounts (HISAs)** are useful if you decide to deal with savings. They offer better rates than many standard bank accounts. Online banking also tends to offer high-interest rates. It also helps you not redraw frequently.

2. **Certificate of Deposits (CDs)** are another great option for savings accounts. There are maturity periods for this type of investment. If one redeems their funds before the maturity date, there are penalties to be paid.

3. **Mutual Funds** are professionally-managed investment schemes, usually run by an asset management company that brings together a group of people and invests their money in stocks, bonds, and other securities.

4. **Roth IRAs** are individual retirement accounts that offer tax-free growth and tax-free withdrawals in retirement. Roth IRA rules dictate that as long as you've owned your account for 5 years and you're age 59½ or older, you can withdraw your money when you want to and you won't owe any federal taxes. A Roth IRA offers tax-free withdrawals. With a Roth IRA, you get a future bonus: every penny you withdraw in retirement stays in your pocket—not Uncle Sam's.

5. **Stocks.** Common stock is ownership in part of a company. The purchaser is entitled to a portion of the company's profit. Stocks provide better returns but with a higher risk.

> As a general rule, when investing, sixty percent of your stock should be in stocks and the rest in bonds.

I'm thankful for my friend Ricardo, who introduced me to the fundamentals of stocks. I signed up for free for a virtual stock trading game on the Investopedia website: virtual money used in buying stocks. This game teaches you how to invest and how to monitor your daily trading before starting to buy your actual stock. Yahoo Finance has a lot of information on trading. It's very important to study about the company, how they have been faring through the years, how many of the board of trustees own shares, and about mergers and future prospects. Stocks that pay dividends are always good. Index is also really good if you can afford it.

6. **Annuities** are contractual financial products sold by financial institutions that are designed to accept and grow funds from an individual and then pay out a stream of payments to the individual at a later point in time. A deferred annuity means that the series of annual payments will not begin until a later date.

7. **Real Estate.** There are many benefits to owning land or real estate. If your goal is good investment returns, then buying a piece of property in a good neighborhood will achieve this goal. Make sure your property is in a location that can be sold easily, not on a major highway or busy street. Check flood zones or, in California, fire zones. Ensure the property is worth the price that it's being sold for. Some people buy a house, live in it for a couple of

years, and then sell it, usually when the market is good and the property has appreciated in value. If you want to generate regular income, then a rental property would be the way to go. Pray for great tenants who will always pay their rent on time. Some buy foreclosure homes for cheap, then fix them and sell them for a higher price. There are some risks in real estate, so you need to do your homework very well. Robert Kiyosaki has great information on this topic; you can research more.

8. **Pay Yourself First.** Whenever you get paid, set aside at least 10% and put it into special savings, a money market account, IRA (ROTH), CD, mutual funds, stocks, or real estate before paying your bills. Make sure these deductions are made automatically into the account you choose. Most companies have a 401k or 403b. If your company matches 100%, make sure you invest the max. Regardless of what the employer matching amount is, contributing the max will help you a lot. You can borrow to invest in real estate or as start-up funds for your business. You can also learn about currency trading; it gives great returns. Spend less than you earn, and save the rest. If you are able to start this at an early age, you will make a lot of money through compounding.

(What is compounding interest? The addition of interest to the principal sum of a loan or deposit is called compounding. Compound interest is interest on interest. It is the result of reinvesting interest, rather than cashing it out, so that interest in the next period is then earned on the principal sum plus previously-accumulated interest.)

Sample Allocation of funds

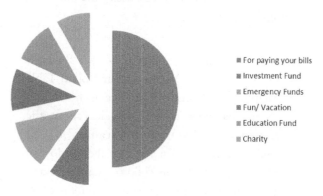

- For paying your bills
- Investment Fund
- Emergency Funds
- Fun/ Vacation
- Education Fund
- Charity

55% paying for your bills

10% Investment Fund (paying yourself first)

10% Emergency Funds

10% Fun / Vacation Fund

10% Education fund

5% Charity

9. **INVEST IN ASSETS NOT LIABILITIES.** Let's briefly look at the difference. Assets produce cash flow to your pocket. Examples include dividend-paying stocks, bonds, businesses, and rental property. A liability produces expenses and does not put money in your pocket. Examples of liabilities are cars, homes (buying a house is great, but rental property is better),

or a boat. You have to be very smart when buying a car; some people buy liabilities (car) just to impress other people. It might be better to invest the money in buying a new car that can yield about 7-12%. The more money you invest in assets, the more money you will make.

10. **Life Insurance.** Franklin Allakpo, a Business Consultant and a Million Dollar Round Table Member, said: "Life insurance is not about the probabilities (death), but it's about the consequences. Do you put a seatbelt on your child because you are going to die, or do you put a seatbelt on your child because the car is going to flip over, or do you put on a seatbelt because of the consequences?"

Life insurance is the most misunderstood product when it comes to our African community or black community as a whole. The oldest product that is guaranteed is permanent Whole Life. The power is not in Whole Life, but the power is in the return of the investment.

In the early '70s, when pensions were in place for many employees, actuary science was part of the equation, but now pensions have been replaced by a 401k/403B for retirement purposes, and actuary science is not part of the equation. Therefore, people are living longer and running out of money in retirement.

Permanent cash value insurance is the only guaranteed product that has actuary science built into it and can provide income for you during retirement when properly structured as long as you live.

If you take an investment profile exam, they usually run a portfolio with traditional Whole Life with fixed income bond or fixed income investment, and the portfolio with Life insurance has less standard deviation, meaning less risk and higher average returns, usually from 7% to 13%.

The Whole Life insurance can be called the Dividend Bible. Inside, you have the ten commandments:

1. The power of compounding.

2. The power of no tax.

3. The power of not losing money.

4. The power of living a legacy for your children's children.

5. The contribution will be made for you by your insurance company if you become disabled and unable to make a payment.

6. You can withdraw money at any time without penalty.

7. No investment fees or brokerage fees.

8. The power of permanency.

9. You have a trusted advisor to watch over it, and he is being paid by the insurance company.

10. The power of guarantee. This is the only investment that is guaranteed in writing. You can partially retire, live in a foreign country, and still be legally getting your dividends, or change your passport or citizenship but still be getting money until the age of 121 years—guaranteed.

The permanent Whole Life insurance contract is an income superstar. A lot of people are ignorant about how permanent life insurance works; we have a bad plan that does not benefit us at all or does not serve as an investment for the middle class.

There was an article published by Ellen E. Schultz May 20th, 2009, in the Wall Street Journal. It revealed how banks are using life insurance to get more returns and to pay the bonuses for the executives. They are racking in a lot of returns while a lot of ordinary people will tell you they don't like insurance and will not even want to talk about it.

According to Paul Essner, permanent life insurance can be a valuable asset class, especially in a volatile market. When used as part of a long-term investment strategy, it provides steady and sustained growth, as well as a tax advantage.

This is an old technique, built on a platform of sustained and steady conservative returns, tax advantages, and a death benefit. But between the late 1990s and 2008, advisers pushed this idea aside in favor of equity-based investment tools— without concern for the impact of volatility and downturn

During the period when stocks and bonds were popular, many advisers overlooked permanent life insurance because it wasn't as exciting or flexible as other asset classes. It wasn't possible to speculate inside a Whole Life policy, and rates of return were seen as unexciting. But as the market turned south, investors who bought Whole Life policies came out ahead. Just as the tortoise beat the hare, the slow and steady returns of life insurance won the race.

Franklin Allakpo informed me he has had clients who've had terrible experiences with their investments in the market but were able to revel in bringing in a 7% or 13% rate of return over a 20- or 30-year period. In those cases, they often said: "I wish I would have bought more." Franklin says he would recommend this approach for clients with a need for life insurance who are generally no older than their mid-50s. If they're older, they might not have the ability to fully benefit from the strategy. So, start investing young, as soon as you get your first job—preferably before your 20th birthday.

Clients using this strategy also need to have sufficient annual income in order to make contributions.

We can conclude that if life insurance is not properly structured, it will be difficult for you to benefit from it. To fully get the best out of it, seek an advisor from a trusted company.

These are some regions with low or no income taxes (these are good locations for investing and starting up businesses).

1. Bahamas	2. Cayman Islands
3. Seychelles	4. Kuwait
5. Panama	6. Bermuda
7. Cyprus	8. Bahrain
9. South Dakota	10. Saudi Arabia
11. Delaware	12. United Arab Emirates
13. Wyoming	14. Qatar
15. Texas	16. Monaco
17. Nevada	18. British Virgin Islands
19. Belize	

It's good to incorporate in states with low taxes or flexible tax laws.

WHEN TOMORROW BECOMES NEVER, DEALING WITH PROCRASTINATION

I thank God you have read up to this point, God bless you.

Why do tomorrow what you can do today? Interestingly, I realize the need to touch on procrastination. Procrastination is the greatest robber of time. We can never get back yesterday, the last hour, or even the last minute.

> **We can never turn back time, and
> thus, we can't afford to waste any of it.**

Does this sound familiar to you? "This is not the right time: too busy, too broke, too stressed, too risky, too uncertain, too inexperienced, too old, too young." Sometimes these reasons make sense, but mostly, they are excuses we use to deal with our fear of failure.

Guess what? Procrastinating year after year does have some level of failure in there, but I hope we can turn it around and start working on your goals right now. I mean, pick up a notepad and write your goals—now. If you never start, you'll never have a chance to fail. But you'll never have a chance to succeed, either.

7 KEYS TO KNOCK OUT PROCRASTINATION

1. **Always write down your goals** and set deadlines; deadlines will push you to work hard and not put it off.

2. **Set small achievable goals.**

> **You don't have to know everything
> before you start. As you move on,
> things will fall into place.**

3. **Visualize the future you want.** Have a picture if you can. Imagination is the key to great achievement. Feed your imagination with where you want to go.

4. **Deal with your fear.**

> One of the saddest discoveries of man
> is to find out he or she can easily do
> what he or she feared to do.

How will you feel a year from now if you don't do what you have always wanted to do?

5. **Build a strong network.** Get a mentor or associate with like-minded people who value what you are pursuing and will always check on how you are progressing in achieving your goals.

6. **Evaluate your progress and celebrate** small successes as you go along. Use your success to drive you to work harder and learn from your mistakes.

7. **Don't quit.** Quitters don't win, and winners don't quit. Speak words of affirmation every day; encourage yourself daily.

If you can't fly, then run; if you can't run, then walk; if you can't walk, then crawl; and if you can't crawl, then drag yourself along. But whatever you do, you have to keep moving forward.

Martin Luther King Jr.

It doesn't matter how fast you are going. As long as you are stepping forward in a direction that is in line with the purpose of God, you are fine. So, take that first step, then another, then another. After all—life rewards action! You are better than those who have not even started. Looking forward to meeting you at the top.

Let's Look at Some High Paying Careers and How to Choose a Profession for The Future

These are just a few of the jobs that Jews encourage their children to go into. They are not afraid to implant wealth and success into their children at an early age. This list does not guarantee success; you always need God on your side and to also follow your passion.

Surgeons	Dentists	Law College Professors
Anesthesiologists	Podiatrists	Air Traffic Controllers
Oral & Maxillofacial Surgeons	Lawyers	Optometrists
Orthodontists	Engineering Managers	Pharmacists

Obstetricians & Gynecologists	Computer & Information systems Managers	Human Resources Managers
Surgeons	Dentist	Law College Professors
Internists	Marketing Managers	Computer & Information Scientists
Family & General Practitioners	Petroleum Engineers	Astronomers
Chief Executives	Airline Pilots/Flight Engineers	Public Relations Managers
Psychiatrists	Financial Managers	Nuclear Engineers
Pediatricians	Physicists	Radiologists

The world is moving at a very fast pace with advanced technology at the forefront; therefore, choosing a career should be done with precision and divine direction. Technology, machines, and robots are gradually replacing manpower.

Let's look at a few trends or changes I have witnessed over the past few years and also what history can teach us.

Ford Automobile is an American corporation that was founded in 1903 by Henry Ford. Ford built his first gasoline-powered horseless carriage, the Quadricycle, in a shed behind his home. The first automobile that was created was powered by steam.

Nicolas-Joseph Cugnot, a French military engineer, built the first steam-powered tricycle for hauling artillery. Before this invention, there were horse-drawn carriages. In the early days of Ford, only a few cars were assembled per day, and they were built by hand by small groups of workers. Ford's mission was to produce an affordable automobile for everyone.

Demand was huge, so Ford developed one of the earliest mass production moving assembly plants. The Ford corporation, through the years, has become one of the strongest family-owned businesses—over 100 years of passing on from one generation to the other. The Ford Company is active and alive today because, through the years, they have kept up with the pace of all the revolutions, technologies, and changes in the automobile industry.

What would have happened if they were still manufacturing horse carriages today? For them to stay in business, they had to continuously find out about future demand and trends, planning for the next ten, twenty, or even thirty years. That is how you stay ahead in any business in these times.

For those of you who remember Blockbuster, it was a huge movie rental franchise located all over the United States. They are no longer in business today. One could rent VHS tapes, DVDs, or video games. This company is out of business because Netflix took over that niche with their technology.

When Netflix first started, they did mail order; now you can watch all their movies in the comfort of your own home. I realize people don't just pay for the movie but the convenience with which they can watch the movie. What should Blockbuster have done? I believe they should have had a dedicated department that always researched product development, new technology, and how to stay in the business.

A lot of companies these days have these departments in their organization. This is what I call buying into the future—that is, always asking God for divine directions. God showed Jacob how he could acquire or restore his lost wealth from his father-in-law.

When the online market explosion started, many people did not feel comfortable about buying something they haven't seen, felt, or tried; look at what has happened now. People order every single thing they use daily—from the Internet.

Today Amazon is a multi-billion-dollar company because it has the largest inventory. They created a platform where there are no racial orientations. Amazon stock is one of the hottest stocks, and I would advise you to invest in that company. That's a layman's advice for buying stock. Anyone can sell or shop online; there is no segregation online, and that's what I love.

Many well-known companies today are closing and going into the online platform. It saves them a lot of money on rental space and employees. You just need a warehouse and a few employees where you will deliver your product from. I believe the delivery industry will boom; there is talk about the use of drones to deliver products, but I think the delivery industry will still be huge.

Computers are replacing many things that humans used to do. One interesting new technology that everyone is talking about these days is artificial intelligence (AI). AI is usually defined as the science of making computers do things that require intelligence when done by humans.

AI has had some success in limited or simplified domains. Machines can do, or will be able to do, a lot of the things humans do faster when programmed. Look at vending machines, self-check-out machines in stores, subway ticket sales, bank tellers, and toll booths. Robots and artificially intelligent software programs are predicted to eliminate a large percentage of jobs in the world, especially in advanced nations. This concern is not just with low-income earners but also with high-income employees.

Retail and manual laborers will also see their job prospects decline. Some of the jobs that could be replaced, or already have been replaced, with AI include:

1. BANK TELLERS

ATMs have taken most human banking jobs, and with the use of smartphone apps, it's likely that many of the remaining human-based teller and representative banking jobs will be taken over by AI soon.

2. FINANCIAL ANALYSTS

Financial analysts would spot investment trends even before it happened; this allowed investment institutions to adjust their portfolios, which could potentially make them millions of dollars. But human financial analysts can no longer compete with artificially intelligent financial analysis software that can read and recognize trends in historical data to predict future market moves. It's no wonder that financial analyst jobs could be the worst hit.

3. CONSTRUCTION WORKERS

Manual labor jobs are very likely be replaced by robotic bricklayers, which can replace two to three human workers and can lay more bricks. I recently saw this technology called SAM (Semi-Automated Mason) on YouTube. Well, humans are still needed to program and make sure the robot functions well.

4. INVENTORY MANAGERS AND STOCKISTS

Robots are replacing the employees at the supermarket warehouses restocking items. The robot is able to audit shelves for out-of-stock items, detecting misplaced items, and pricing errors. This kind of technology is going to be huge and lucrative for business owners because, unlike humans, these robots don't get sick and no payment, retirement, or 401k is needed.

5. FARMERS

Farmers are being replaced by artificially intelligent robots that can do everything from milking cows to pulling lettuce. According to Modern Farmer, a family-owned dairy farm in Germany was one of the first to install Voluntary Milking

System robots that allowed cows to walk up to the machines at their leisure when they wanted to be milked. And more than one million of the U.S.'s farmhands could see their jobs replaced by intelligent machines that do everything from weed cabbage patches to picking apples, reports Quartz.

6. TAXI DRIVERS

Driving jobs could face a hit too, with the introduction of autonomous vehicles. It shouldn't be surprising to know that even Uber or Lyft are investing in self-driving taxis, without paying the driver, so that they increase their profit margin. This system has already begun in Singapore.

7. MANUFACTURING WORKERS

The human manufacturing workforce will be hugely affected; robots again will be replacing the manpower needed. As a matter of fact, it's already happening. Foxconn, Samsung, and most Chinese manufacturers that are into iPhones and Xboxes recently replaced over 60,000 workers with robots.

As I work on this final chapter, I am praying and thinking about future jobs; the Lord laid this information on my heart, and I wanted to share it with you. It will be very difficult for robots to replace nurses and doctors. The healthcare industry will be pretty strong for a long time, as machines and robots are replacing most of the manpower. Technicians, who will be servicing and maintaining these robot's hardware and software, will be in great demand. Online marketing has come to stay with drones delivering packages; therefore, web security and maintenance will be a priority for most companies.

Finally, my dear reader, we have all been given a large blackboard and chalk; you have the right to write your life story. What will you write? You are alive this moment; that's why you are reading this book. It's never too late to start. Age, they say, is just a number. Let's go, start your journey, and we will all meet at the top. Cheers!

I thank God for these people whose knowledge, support, and love, directly or indirectly, helped me immensely in writing this book.

My parents Mr. & Mrs. Bediako; Mr. & Mrs. Kyei Mensah; Rebecca Aidoo; siblings: Vatraut, Victoria, Helmut, and Afuah Kyei; Jesse Morgan and the Morgan family; Yaw Gyasi; Emmanuel Barko Boafo; Pastor Nicholas Ankamah; Bishop Amo Brown; Apostle Ben Paul; Rev. Francis Yost; Robert Kiyosaki; Pastor Harrison Acheampong; Nathan's Family; Celia Cunningham; Efehe Williams; Ricardo; Mariam .S; my lovely big sister first lady Kirby Assuo Mensah; Apostle Ami Narh; MOBA 95; Pastor Azigiza; Kwasi Koomson; Rev. & First lady Shalders; Pastor Daniel Donkor; Ps. Adu Gyamfi; Denise Robinson; Edinam Cudjoe; Linda Liverpool; Pastor Kwame Acheampong; Pastor Steve Paintsil; Yaw Ansong; Yaw Osei; Kofi Boye; Kwamina Acheampong; Steven Koranteng; Simflex Nyame; Samuel Akufo; and Pastor Owusu Bempah.

Dr. C. Thomas Anderson, the author of "Becoming a Millionaire God's Ways," Zig Ziggler, Myles Monroe, Maya Angelou, Van Moody, TD Jakes, and H.W. Charles.

References:

https://www.fastcompany.com/3067279/you-didnt-see-this-coming-10-jobs-that-will-be-replaced-by-robots
www.history.com
Forbes 2016 report
www.investopedia.com

Interested in starting your own online business?

Visit this site:
www.surge365.com/royalediscounttravel
Looking for business ideas?
https://www.entrepreneur.com/businessideas
https://businesstown.com/businessopps/newbiz.asp
Recommended Books:
"The Business You Can Start" & "Workbook" by Victor Kwegyir
"Beyond The Passion" by Victor Kwegyir

How to get funding for businesses:

www.fundable.com
www.kickstarter.com
www.getfunded.com
www.gogetfunding.com
www.gofundme.com
Recommended Book:
"Pitch Your Business Like a Pro" by Victor Kwegyir

Good sites for self-education:

www.investopedia.com/university
www.bloomberg.com/markets

Made in the USA
Middletown, DE
10 March 2022